THE SECOND WORLD WAR IN I

1941

JOHN CHRISTOPHER & CAMPBELL McCUTCHEON

AMBERLEY

First published 2014

Amberley Publishing
The Hill, Stroud
Gloucestershire, GL5 4EP

www.amberley-books.com

British Library Cataloguing in Publication Data.
A catalogue record for this book is available from the British Library.

ISBN 978 1 4456 2209 5 (print)
ISBN 978 1 4456 2225 5 (ebook)

Typeset in 11pt on 15pt Sabon.
Typesetting and Origination by Amberley Publishing.
Printed in the UK.

Contents

Introduction

1941 began with the Germans planning their offensive against Russia, fighting in the Western Desert between British and Italians and a continuance of the sea war in the Atlantic. The conflict was still contained within Europe and North Africa, but events in the Pacific later in the year, as well as the invasion of Russia, would turn the tide of the war and bring the two biggest nations in the world into the fray.

With heavy losses in the Battle of the Atlantic, President Roosevelt announces on 2 January that American shipyards would build 200 cargo ships, to be known as 'Liberty' ships. These ships were to a standard design, using as much prefabricated steel as possible, and were designed to be simple and easy to construct, with much welding and little riveting. The design itself was British but, between 1941 and 1945, the number of ships built would exceed 2,710 in eighteen different American shipyards.

General Sir Archibald Wavell's Middle East Force begins an assault on the Italians on 3 January in Cyrenaica. Australian land-based troops make their first major offensive of the war as they attack and capture Bardia on 15 January, along with some 70,000 Italian troops and much of their equipment. Between 7 and 22 January, the British 7th Armoured Brigade surrounds Tobruk, Libya. The Australian 6th Division again leads the final assault and Tobruk capitulates on 22 January. The Allies gain an important port, complete with much of its equipment, as well as vital stores of food, fuel and water, as well as 30,000 Italian prisoners. Forces are immediately sent westwards to capture the port of Benghazi. The Italians are also under threat in East Africa, when, on 19 January, British forces push out from the Sudan into Eritrea. Meanwhile, in Libya, the British 4th Armoured Brigade attacks the Italians around Mechili, dividing the Italian troops between Mechili and Derna, and makes attempts to encircle both sets of enemy forces. The pressure is kept on the Italian troops in Africa, with the invasion of Italian Somaliland from Kenya on 29 January. In Washington, on the same day, the Americans agree that if they enter the war, the German defeat is the principal aim of a combined US-British force in Europe. In March, as a direct result of the talks, an American mission comes to Britain to survey possible bases for US forces on land, sea and air.

On 1 February, the US Navy is split into three distinct forces, Atlantic, Pacific and Asiatic fleets, with much strengthening of the Atlantic fleet to cope with the

The bow of a Liberty ship is craned into place before welding at Terminal Island, California. These ships were constructed to a standard design, using as much prefabricated steel as possible, and were designed to be simple and easy to construct, with much welding and little riveting. Although a British design, the number of ships built would exceed 2,710 in eighteen different American shipyards.

demands of submarine warfare, as well as the threat of German surface raiders. Based in Brest, the *Admiral Hipper*, a German cruiser, makes constant forays into the Atlantic, successfully attacking Allied convoys, between 1 February and March, when she returns unobserved to Kiel for an overhaul via the Denmark Strait. The two battlecruisers *Scharnhorst* and *Gneisenau* leave port on 3 February and also cause havoc in the Atlantic, sinking twenty-two ships between then and 22 March, when they return to France once more. Between 5 and 7 February, the Italians are totally surrounded south of Benghazi and surrender to the British 7th Armoured Division, while the Australian 6th Division takes the surrender of Benghazi on 7 February. The numerically inferior Allied forces have defeated a larger army by using land, sea and air forces in conjunction with each other. The Bulgarians effectively enter the war on the Axis side on 14 February by allowing German access to their border with Greece. In Russia, General Zukhov becomes chief of the General Staff, while the Germans send a division of armoured troops to ensure the Italians do not withdraw from Libya. They disembark in Tripoli on Valentine's Day. With a crisis occurring in Greece, the Allied leaders and Greek government agree that 100,000 British troops will embark for Greece. On 25 February, British troops enter Mogadishu, Somaliland, as the defeated Italians leave their one-time colony.

On 1 March, Bulgaria officially enters the war on the Axis side and Free French forces take the Italian airbase at the oasis of Kufra after besieging the area for twenty-two days. British and Norwegian commandos attack the Lofoten islands on 4 March, destroying fish-oil processing factories that are used to make ingredients for explosives. Capturing 215 Germans, they also rescue 300 Norwegians and take them back to the UK. Ten ships are sunk in the daring raid too. British troops sail from Port Said and Alexandria for the Balkans on 5 March and by the beginning of April there are 58,000 British troops in Greece. With major defeats in Africa, Mussolini tries to take some glory and attacks Greece between 9 and 25 March. The attacks from Albania are met with stiff Greek defence and fail. 11 March sees Roosevelt signing the Lend Lease Act, allowing Britain to pay later for weapons, munitions, vehicles and other supplies. Britain can and does pay its way for the whole of 1941. By 24 March, the German Afrika Korps attacks the British at El Agheila, signalling the start of a campaign by the Afrika Korps and its enigmatic leader Erwin Rommel that will continue all year. The German tanks race across the desert towards Tobruk to ensure another port for the German supply route.

In the east, Yugoslavia enters the war and joins the Axis powers on 25 March. Two days later, a coup takes place and Prince Paul's pro-Axis government is overthrown. As a result, and with the Italian attack on Greece stalled, Hitler issues Directive No. 25, authorising the invasion of Yugoslavia and of Greece too. Both are scheduled to occur simultaneously on 6 April. The Italians suffer more bad news in Africa as they are defeated at the Battle of Keren on 27 March. Their forces in Eritrea flee for Asmara, which is captured less than a week later. The bad news continues for the Italians, who send their battle fleet into the Aegean on 28 March. Hoping to disrupt British troop convoys to Greece, they meet with a British naval force under Admiral Henry Pridham-Wippell. Retreating, the Italians hope to escape from the larger British

At the end of 1940, President Roosevelt had declared that the USA would become the 'Arsenal of Democracy'. At the time this meant supplying the British and Allies with military equipment under the Lend-Lease policy, which came into effect on 11 March 1941. But before the year was out the Japanese attack on Pearl Harbor would bring America into the war as a full combatant. *Above:* Douglas DB-7 bombers on the assembly line in California. *Below:* M4 medium tanks being mass-produced at the Chrysler Tank Arsenal in Warren, Detroit.

force they know must be nearby. Two torpedo bombers from the aircraft carrier *Formidable* attack the Italian cruisers and battleships, damaging the *Vittorio Veneto* and the cruiser *Pola*. Three British battleships attack the *Pola* and her escorts and by 29 March, there are five Italian ships sunk, with the loss of 3,000 crew. The British lose a single aircraft at the Battle of Cape Matapan. The end of the month sees the American government confiscating sixty-five Axis ships in their ports and harbours.

In the Middle East, Iraq's regent Faisal is overthrown by pro-Axis forces at the beginning of April. With their oil supplies endangered, British troops arrive on 18 April to safeguard the oil. In North Africa, by the 4th, the Germans and Italians under Rommel advance across Libya to retake Benghazi and Msus. Directive No. 25 is enacted and thirty-three German divisions, with support from the Italians and Hungarians, invade Yugoslavia, Between 10 and 15 April, Zagreb, Belgrade and Sarajevo are captured and the 640,000-strong Yugoslav army is defeated. Simultaneous attacks on Greece see the destruction of a British ammunition ship in Piraeus harbour, causing thirteen other ships to be sunk in the resultant explosion. By 9 April, the Greek 2nd Army surrenders after being cut off in Salonika. The British are forced back to a new line at Mount Olympus as the Greek forces on their left collapse. As the Greeks are routed, the Italians in Ethiopia retreat from the capital, Addis Ababa, after British troops advance 1,000 miles from Kenya and defeat them. By 9 April, the port of Massawa is captured, along with seventeen vessels. Rommel, in Libya, defeats British troops at Derna, capturing the important town on 7 April. As Yugoslavia falls apart under the Axis invasion, Croatia declares independence on 10 April. Greenland is occupied by the Americans, who help the British set up weather stations in the Danish colony. The weather stations will help the British keep informed of weather conditions that will hit Europe some four days after their observation in Greenland. The siege of Tobruk begins on 10 April. Tobruk is the only major port for 1,000 miles between Alexandria and Sfax, in Tunisia, and is bitterly defended by the Allies, who cannot afford to lose the strategic port. The Russians and Japanese, who have been in conflict in Manchuria, since the mid-1930s, sign a non-aggression pact on 13 April 1941. This helps the Russians, who can move many troops from Siberia to the west in expectation of a German attack, and the Japanese too, who are already preparing for their attacks against the Americans, Dutch, French and British in Asia and the Pacific.

17 April sees Yugoslavia agree an armistice with the Axis and the country comes under German control apart from the puppet state of Croatia. Yugoslav resistance begins almost immediately. The Greek troops are in trouble and British reinforcements from Egypt are cancelled on 18 April. An evacuation of British troops seems likely and is as much as confirmed as the Greeks surrender in Albania on 20 April. British forces abandon their positions around Thermopylae on 24 April and head to ports and beaches in eastern Greece. Some 43,000 are rescued under heavy German fire. Two destroyers and four troop transports are lost. Athens is occupied on 27 April, while the Greek parliament makes for Crete. Dead in the invasion for Greece are 15,700 Greeks, 13,755 Italians, 1,518 Germans and 900 British troops. 640 bombers attack Plymouth on the nights of 21/22 and

29/30 April, with the loss of 750 lives and leaving 30,000 people homeless. Führer Directive No. 28 is issued on 25 April and is key to the invasion of Crete, which is codenamed Operation Mercury. A major offensive against Tobruk begins on 30 April. Within four days, the Axis troops secure positions on the south-west of the defences but it is obvious the Allied troops will not easily be shifted. The siege begins in earnest with the Allies' only means of supply by sea. They will be harried by German and Italian submarines, torpedo boats and aircraft in the coming months.

In Iraq, German bombers help the Iraqi forces against the British, who are soon reinforced. The last major stand by the Italians in East Africa takes place between 3 and 19 May, as the Battle of Amba Alagi settles who will have control of East Africa. The British victory means that 230,000 Italians have been killed or captured and that the Italian empire in East Africa is now no more. The Allies have complete control of the Red Sea, safeguard Egypt and retain a safe route into North Africa via the Suez Canal. During the last ditch attempts by the Italians to retain Ethiopia, Emperor Haile Selassie returns triumphantly after five years in exile. Operation Tiger, the first of many Gibraltar to Egypt convoys through the Mediterranean, brings supplies to Egypt to support a British desert offensive. Using the entire Mediterranean Fleet, another two convoys also leave Egypt for Gibraltar. The five ships of Tiger are attacked while on the way across the Mediterranean and one is sunk by a mine, taking fifty-seven tanks to the bottom. A further 238 tanks and forty-three Hurricanes make it safely to Egypt on 12 May. Two days earlier, Rudolf Hess had set off for Britain in a Messerschmitt Bf 110. Hess is the second in command in Nazi Germany and he thinks the British will agree to a plan that will see the British Empire left intact, while Germany controls Europe. He is swiftly imprisoned and replaced by Martin Bormann. The night of 10/11 May sees 507 German bombers attack London. This will be the last major raid on London for another three years. Between September 1940 and May 1941, many British towns and cities had been pounded nightly with nearly 40,000 deaths.

In Africa, Operation Brevity sees the Allies attack the Afrika Korps and push them back, capturing Halfaya Pass and Sollum between 15 and 16 May. The build-up to the invasion of Crete begins with constant air attacks on the island by the Luftwaffe. An airborne invasion signals the start of the main attack on 20 May. It is the first major airborne invasion in history and involves nearly 23,000 soldiers, who are up against 43,000 British, New Zealand, Australian and Greek troops. Before being forced to withdraw, the British fleet manages to sink numerous German troop transports, and 5,000 die. On 23 May, the German ships *Bismarck* and *Prinz Eugen* are located by the County-class cruisers *Norfolk* and *Suffolk* in the Denmark Strait between Iceland and Greenland. Being trailed by HMS *Hood* and HMS *Prince of Wales*, Bismarck destroys the *Hood*, with the loss of almost all her crew, while severely damaging the *Prince of Wales*. The *Bismarck* is damaged and her oil tanks begin to leak. Making for Brest, *Bismarck* is lost and aircraft from the *Ark Royal* find her again, damaging her steering. Two battleships pound the German vessel, with shells from the *Rodney* and *King George V* turning the *Bismarck* into a burning hulk before she sinks. While the Germans lose the

Above: A British pilot clambers out of the cockpit of an American-built Grumman Martlet.

Bismarck, they have all but overrun Crete, with the British evacuation taking place at the end of the month. Losses in the battle for Crete are comparative with about 3,700–3,900 dead on each side. Under air attack, 15,000 Allied troops are rescued. On 30 May, Iraq agrees an armistice with Britain and in an embarrassing accident, Germany bombs neutral Eire on 31 May, causing twenty-eight deaths in Dublin.

As the Germans consolidate their victory in Crete, an Allied force of 20,000 Free French, British and Commonwealth troops begins the preparations for the invasion of Syria from Palestine. The invasion begins on 8 June amid spirited defence by the Vichy French, who soon have naval support on 9 June. By 21 June, Damascus has been captured. Operation Battleaxe is launched on 15 June to relieve Tobruk but new tanks prove unreliable and, after the loss of ninety of 190 tanks, the offensive is called off on 17 June. After delays caused by the invasion of Greece, Germany launches Operation Barbarossa on 22 June 1940. Along a 2,000-mile front, some 3 million Germans invade. The plan is simple and involves a Blitzkrieg style attack and a quick victory over the Russians, with consolidation and mopping up over the winter. In the north and centre, German soldiers, assisted by their Axis allies, make steady progress but in the south they are slowed by severe fighting. The Russians lose 1,800 aircraft at the start of Barbarossa. Soon, the Finns enter the war, declaring war on Russia on 26 June with the aim of retaking land lost after the winter war of 1939/40. Between 26 and 30 June, Brest Litovsk is taken and the river Bug is crossed. With aerial superiority, the Germans simply bypass resistance, encircling Bialystok, Novogrudock and Volkovysk. With the Germans rapidly advancing, Hungary declares war on 27 June.

July begins with an advancing German army crossing the river Dvina and the Berezina. Attempts are being made to cross the Dniepr to aid the race for Moscow. In Ethiopia, on 3 June, the 7,000 Italians remaining surrender and on 7 June, the US Army occupies Iceland. After years of being on opposing sides, Britain and Russia sign a Mutual Assistance pact on 12 July. On the same day, Moscow is attacked from the air by the Luftwaffe. Three large attacks take place in July and numerous other air raids take place throughout the year. Syria surrenders to the Allies on 14 July after the loss of around 6,000 combatants of both sides. Two days later, Smolensk is encircled and 300,000 Russian troops are trapped, along with 3,200 tanks. Fighting continues until the end of August, using valuable German resources needed for the advance to Moscow. The southern arm of the German advance is stuck in the Pripet Marshes and General Guderian's Panzer army is shifted south to help against the Soviet 5th Army. This troop movement removes some of the men needed for the attack on Moscow.

The resupply of Malta begins on 21 July, with convoys sent to the beleaguered island with fuel, food and ammunition to fight the Italians and Germans. After a month of fighting, the German Army Group North halts south of Leningrad to rest from the rigors of fighting a spirited Russian defence. This gives the Soviets time to bring in reinforcements and strengthen positions in front of Moscow and Leningrad. Army Group South tries to close the gap around Uman, in the Ukraine. Two weeks later, some 100,000 Russian soldiers and 317 tanks are trapped, with supply only by sea. Between 26 and 29 July, the USA and UK freeze Japanese assets in their countries, with the Japanese taking a tit-for-tat approach. At the end of the month, Reinhard Heydrich begins the implementation of the Final Solution. Many Jews are already in camps or ghettos and have been persecuted since war began, and before in Germany. In Vichy France, some 13,000 have been interned since June.

August sees the USA ban exports of oil to Japan, which relies on imports to survive. Japan must either change its expansionist foreign policy or invade an oil-rich Pacific neighbour. On 5 August, a seventy-three-day siege of Odessa begins. Using the Dniepr as a defensive line, the Russians spend time removing industry to the other side of the Urals and destroying all in the Germans' path in a scorched earth policy. German objectives are changed by Führer Directive No. 34, issued on 12 August. The attack on Moscow is halted, while attacks are made towards Leningrad and the rich agricultural and industrial country of the Ukraine. 6,000 Australian troops leave Tobruk and are swapped for 6,000 Poles. The Soviets begin withdrawing their troops across the Dniepr on 18 August. Hitler's attempts to trap many of the Soviets have left many areas where the retreating Russians can still pass. Meanwhile, in the far north, the first Arctic convoy leaves for Archangel with vital military aid on 21 August, arriving there in ten days. The German encirclement of Kiev begins on 23 August. British and Soviet troops invade Iran on 25 August to ensure any pro-German sympathies are crushed and to secure vital oil installations. A Soviet counter-offensive begins on 30 August but this fails.

September begins with German forces attacking Leningrad, being within a few miles of the city, and they besiege the city for over 1,000 days. On the second anniversary of the declaration of war by Britain, a new gas is used in a little-known Polish internment camp called Auschwitz. Chambers are built to test out the gas, called Zyklon-B, which proves to be successful. The widespread use of the gas to

Below: British guns defending the beleagured city of Tobruk in Lybia, 1941. The fighting in North Africa opened up a new war front known by the Germans as the Southern Front.

A small boat rescues a sailor from the USS *West Virginia*. Inboard is the USS *Tennessee*. Ordinarily, at Pearl Harbor, the battleships alternated being out on patrol. Six would be out with Task Force One and then the following week another three would be out with the aircraft carrier task force. The task force required speed and the battleships were too slow so none were out on the morning of 7 December. USS *Nevada* was able to move during the attack but was hit by a torpedo as she raised steam. Her crew shot down four bombers that morning.

kill 'undesirables' is rolled out. Mistaken for a British destroyer, the USS *Greer* is attacked by a U-boat on 4 September. This causes the Americans to order their warships to shoot on sight in waters important to national defence. 6 September sees the introduction of laws requiring Jews to wear the Star of David. Freedom of movement is also restricted. 500,000 Russian soldiers are trapped on 15 September when 2nd Panzer Group and Army Group South meet at Lokhvitsa, 100 miles east of Kiev. It is the end for the Soviet South West Front. Having been delayed from leaving Kiev by Stalin, the Soviet forces begin a fighting withdrawal from Kiev. By the 19th, their escape routes are cut off and Kiev is seized with the loss of 665,000 men. On 24 June, the first German U-boat enters the Mediterranean, while Operation Halberd, a convoy for Malta, leaves Gibraltar. On 29 September, 33,771 Jews are killed in Kiev. In the south of Ukraine, 1st Panzer Group severs a vital railway line on 30 September. The advance to Rostov encircles 106,000 Russian troops and 212 tanks on 6 October. 29 September also sees the final push to Moscow, Operation Typhoon, with seventy-three German divisions up against eight-five Soviet divisions.

Between 6 and 15 October, Germany's Second Army and Second Panzer Army encircle three Soviet armies near Bryansk and 35,000 Soviet troops are evacuated from Odessa on 15 October. 8 October sees heavy rains ahead of Moscow and these turn the roads into muddy, impassable tracks. The Germans spend their time mopping up resistance in the Bryansk pocket. Despite capturing 673,000 men and 1,242 tanks, the Russians have time to create new defensive positions in front of Moscow. Japanese attempts to appease the Americans have failed and on 16 October, Prince Konoye is replaced as Prime Minister by General Tojo, the Defence Minister. The pro-war faction is in control of Japan and the attacks against America are soon to come. Moscow is under siege! Joseph Stalin orders defences built around the Russian capital. The whole population is mobilised and all resources of use to the Germans are destroyed if they cannot be moved ahead of occupation. The Russians will be saved not by the efforts of their population but by the weather. With deteriorating weather conditions, the Germans change the objectives of Operation Typhoon. Greece, the Ukraine and a stubborn Russian defence has caused the Axis offensive to falter and slow. Despite the huge gains, the massive numbers of men captured, the material acquired, the Russians keep on coming and their huge natural resources ensure they will keep fighting. Mobilisation of the Russian people is well under way. On 24 October, the German Sixteenth Army enters Kharhov, which has already been abandoned by the Russians. At the end of the month, the US destroyer *Rueben James* is sunk by a U-boat, with the loss of 100 American sailors.

Fighting in the Ukraine is still heavy, and on 1 November, the Wehrmacht launches an offensive on the Don at Rostov. Attempts at encirclement fail and the Germans do take Rostov on 21 November but it is recaptured by the Russians on 29 November. General von Rundstedt resigns after ignoring Hitler's instructions and making a tactical withdrawal. On 6 November, the Russians are granted a $1 billion loan from the USA. More U-boats have reached the Mediterranean and on

13 November, two attack the aircraft carriers *Ark Royal* and *Argus*, which have been flying off fighters for Malta and are en route back to Gibraltar. *Ark Royal* is badly damaged and 25 miles from Gibraltar, she catches fire and sinks, taking seventy aircraft to the bottom. The weather is now taking its toll on the German soldiers, who are ill-equipped for the Russian winter. The Soviets, however, are prepared and are being supplied with brand new T-34 tanks. By the end of the month, the Germans are halted only 20 miles from Moscow. The war in Libya continues apace – Operation Crusader, the latest attempt to break through to Tobruk, occurs between 18 and 26 November – with the British light tanks suffering mechanical issues. Engagements with the Germans at Sidi Rezegh and Italians within Tobruk went in the favour of the Allies though and they relieve some of the pressure on their besieged port. 26 November would see the turning point of the war. A Japanese fleet leaves the Kurile Islands on a mission so important, the Japanese are prepared to risk everything on its results. That fleet, of six aircraft carriers, two battleships, three cruisers, nine destroyers, three submarines and eight tankers, is to change the world forever. However, the idea for its mission has come from the British. In November 1940, the Fleet Air Arm had proved that you could sink many warships at their base, in shallow water, in the dark, using nothing more than a few stringbag aircraft, made of wood, cloth and armed solely with an 1880s invention, a torpedo. Taranto can be considered the model for the attack the Japanese have set their whole country's future on. The Italian naval base was attacked by aircraft of the Fleet Air Arm and one battleship was sunk, two severely damaged and a cruiser damaged too, all for the cost of two aircraft. December will be a month of surprises. Meanwhile, on 28 November, the last Italians in Ethiopia surrender, some 20,000 captured at Gondar. U-208 is sunk in the Bay of Biscay by the first aircraft to use air-surface radar successfully.

December is a month of declarations of war! Britain declares war on Finland, Hungary and Romania on 6 December. Of course, it is just a gesture and Britain will not enter combat with these nations at this point in the war. The next day brings a rather nasty shock for the Americans and the British. The Japanese fleet which had sailed from the Kurile Islands is close to Hawaii. 183 aircraft fly off the carriers and attack the home of the US Navy's Pacific Fleet at Pearl Harbor. The targets are the aircraft carriers but, unknown to the Japanese, these are out on exercise. Nonetheless, six battleships are destroyed, ten other vessels are damaged or lost, and 188 aircraft destroyed too. Japanese losses are five midget submarines and twenty-nine aircraft. In an accident of timing, the Japanese declare war on America and the British Commonwealth after the attack has started. This causes outrage in the USA. A planned third wave of aircraft, which are to destroy the oil terminals and harbour, is called off as the Japanese do not want to risk their carriers.

Hitler issues Führer Directive No. 39 on 8 December. He calls off the advance on Moscow for the winter. Army Group Centre pulls back, much to the Führer's fury. Declarations of war are made too on this day. America, Britain, New Zealand, Australia, Holland, the Free French and Yugoslavia declare war on Japan, as do several South American countries. The world is now truly at war. China too

Above: In December 1941, Adolf Hitler assumed command of the German army following Field Marshal Von Brauchitsch's resignation after a heart attack.

declares war on the Axis states. Rommel pulls his forces back from Tobruk and the siege is over. 8 December also sees Japanese invasions of the Philippines, Hong Kong, Malaya and Thailand. These attacks actually happen within hours of the attack on Pearl Harbor but, being across the International Date Line, they are recorded as a full day later in the history books. The attack on the Philippines sees 100 American aircraft destroyed at Clark Field and an attack on Luzon Island on the 10th. Guam and Wake are soon captured. Hong Kong refuses the Japanese surrender terms on 13 December and will finally capitulate on Christmas Day. 100,000 Japanese invade Malaya and Thailand and start to work their way down the Malay peninsula. With many of the British troops stationed at Singapore, with its great naval base, progress is swift. By the time the British troops get to Thailand it is too late to repulse the Japanese landings. On 10 December, the futility of sending battleships into war without adequate air cover is finally realised as both HMS *Repulse* and *Prince of Wales* are destroyed by around ninety Japanese aircraft. 730 die in the tragic waste of both ships, leaving Britain with no battleships in this part of the Pacific.

Both Germany and Italy declare war on America on 11 December, with Romania following on 12 December. The USA's involvement in the European war is now guaranteed. 13 December is an unlucky day for the Italians, but a huge success for the Allies when they sink two Italian fast cruisers taking fuel to North Africa. 900 die in the waters off Sicily. The attack has been made by three British and one Dutch destroyer. HMS *Urge* torpedoes two Italian transports carrying stores for Libya and damages the battleship *Vittorio Veneto* off Messina to round off a successful day in the Mediterranean. The next day, a convoy of thirty-two ships sails from Gibraltar for Britain. Among the escorts is the escort carrier HMS *Audacity*, the first of Britain's new vessels designed to provide support to convoys without the range of land-based aircraft. U-boat wolf packs are operating and the convoy encounters twelve enemy submarines, sinking five, but for the loss of *Audacity*, a destroyer and two merchant ships. Despite her loss, *Audacity* has shown her usefulness and soon many convoys will operate with these smaller escort carriers. Twenty-eight of the original thirty-two ships reach Britain on 23 December. Borneo is invaded on 16 December and British and Dutch forces destroy the oil installations before retreating. Between 18 and 19 December, the Italians avenge the loss of their ships on the 13th. Force K runs into an enemy minefield and HMS *Neptune* and *Kandahar* are lost. Two cruisers are damaged too. However, the worst damage of the day occurs in Alexandria. Italian 'human torpedoes' sink two battleships. HMS *Queen Elizabeth* and HMS *Valiant* sink in shallow water and are ultimately repaired but their loss changes the balance of power in the Mediterranean. The British soon copy the idea, which involves two frogmen and a tiny submersible containing a huge warhead, and we shall see the effects later in the war.

In what will ultimately become his costliest mistake in the war, Adolf Hitler assumes command of the Germany Army on 19 December, following Field Marshal Von Brauchitsch's resignation after a heart attack. In the Philippines, Japanese forces invade Mindanao on 20 December, along with Jolo. The main invasion of Luzon begins on 22 December and General MacArthur retreats from Manila to Bataan, declaring the city open. Churchill and Roosevelt meet on 22 December in Washington. It is now that agreements to build up US forces in Britain are made. Churchill offers Roosevelt the *Queen Mary* and *Queen Elizabeth*, Britain's largest ships, in a reverse Lend-Lease deal and these will bring US Divisions to Fortress Britain. Between 26 and 28 December, commandos attack the Lofoten Islands, with 260 troops destroying a vital fish-oil plant on Boxing Day. A second landing the next day will see 600 troops destroy more fish plants and radio stations. Hitler is convinced that Britain will attack and invade Norway and sends more troops and aircraft to protect the country from the perceived invasion. These troops will ultimately be tied up for the duration of the war, preventing them from fighting where they were really needed.

All in all, 1941 is a successful year for the Allies, but only in hindsight. At the time, it still looks bleak for the Allies. Britain is finally safe from invasion though, while the war in Africa has seen huge victories in the East, but in the North, the war has swung both ways. Japan's drawing of America into the war has unleashed the world's most powerful country from its slumber and the industrial power of the USA, combined with the sheer population and size of Russia, will ultimately turn the tide of the war. With Pearl Harbor, the Japanese have won a great tactical victory but have lost the war even as it starts. There will be no short war, as they hope, but a long drawn out affair that will only end in defeat for the Axis nations.

JANUARY 1941

A transatlantic convoy photographed in 1941. By 1940, the Germans were sinking as many ships in a month as the British could build, creating a problem that could only be solved by construction in US yards of ships that were simple to build and repair after war damage. These were the Liberty ships.

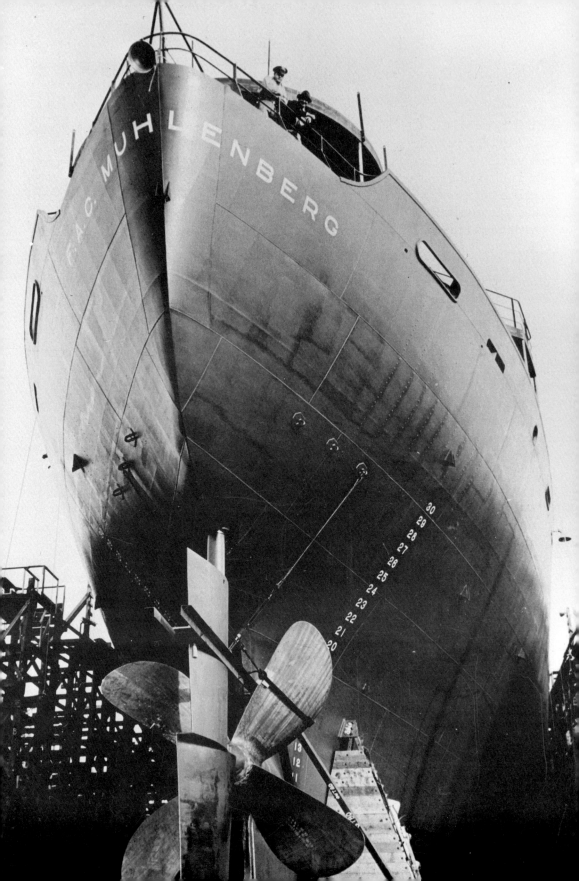

The Liberty Ship – Saviour of the Battle of the Atlantic

The *John W. Brown* and the *Jeremiah O'Brien* remain today as the only two operational examples of the 2,710 vessels of the EC2-S-C1 class of ships built between 1941 and 1945, which we know as the Liberty ships. For a ship with a design life of five years, and built in wartime, to still have two afloat and in service over seventy years later is not bad going. Based on a British design, this was modified by the United States Maritime Commission to make the ships easier and cheaper to build. They were as standardised as possible, and with a length of around 441 feet and a displacement of 14,245 tons, they could carry over 10,000 tons of cargo. With a speed of 11.5 kt, they could steam for 20,000 nautical miles using their two oil-fired boilers to power simple reciprocating steam engines that proved reliable and easy to repair. Fitted with various machine guns, they also sported a stern-mounted 4-inch gun for defence against submarines.

Eighteen shipyards supplied the ships and eighteen builders the engines, and the ships were designed to be put together as fast as the components came into the shipyard. Ordinarily, a ship would go from keel laying to launching in less than a month, with completion down to forty-two days by the end of the war.

The Liberty ships played a vital part in the Battle of the Atlantic and it is only the speed of construction of so many ships that saved Britain from starvation during 1942. The first American ship to sink a German surface vessel was the SS *Stephen Hopkins*, in 1942, when she destroyed the commerce raider *Stier* in a gun battle. One notable survivor is to be found off the coast of Kent, the SS *Richard Montgomery*, which sank off the Medway Approach Channel on 20 August 1944, while carrying thousands of tons of ammunition. Breaking her back, she was part salvaged but still to this day contains 1,400 tons of TNT in the bombs she still contains. One Liberty ship that did explode, the SS *E. A. Bryan*, blew up after 2,000 tons of TNT went off in July 1944. 320 sailors and civilians died.

The design was flawed and some Liberty ships developed stress fractures and three broke in half. It was discovered that the temperature of the Atlantic made the steel used brittle. 2,400 survived the war and many became the backbone of many shipping fleets. In 1965, 165 Liberty ships were mothballed by the US as part of their strategic defence. Numerous examples still survive, with the two in steam today. Other notable survivors include the Greek SS *Arthur M. Huddell*, while two remain in Portland, Oregon, as floating dry docks. Another, the SS *Albert M. Boe*, survives as a land-locked cannery in Kodiak, Alaska. For a five-year planned use, the numbers that have survived and that continued in service even into the 1970s are, frankly, amazing. The Liberty ships were joined by a few other standard designs, including Victory ships and oil tankers, many destined to give as valuable service after the war's end as they did during the war itself.

Opposite page: The use of standardised parts meant that the ships could speedily be built. This view shows the rudder and propeller of a Liberty ship prior to launch in California.

Above: What made the design possible was the use of welding rather than riveting, which could speed the construction, as well as use much less steel than a riveted ship. Here, welders stitch together parts of the hull of the Liberty ship SS *Frederick Douglass* at the Bethlehem-Fairfield yard in Maryland.

Opposite page, top: Built in American shipyards, the Liberty ships were supplied to Britain on a Lend-Lease basis. The might of American industrialisation would go on to produce thousands of this standard design. *Opposite bottom:* Supplies for Russia, which entered the war in June 1941, were sent either to Murmansk and Archangel in the frozen north or via Iran and into southern Russia. Here, a Liberty ship unloads in an Iranian port.

Launched and in the water at the Bethlehem-Fairfield yard, Maryland, by the time the war ended over 2,700 Liberty ships had been built. Many survived the war and two are in active preservation today.

Right: Two Liberty ships during their final fitting out at an East Coast shipyard. The ease of construction and speed of delivery ensured the industrial might of the USA would help win the war. A similar design was available for tankers and, as a result of the use of the Liberty ships, a new design came into being called the Victory class.

Below: A convoy later in the war, with numerous Liberty ships making up parts of the convoy.

Above: German and Italian naval officers meet to discuss their tactics in the offensive against Britain's Atlantic shipping. Admiral Raeder, Commander-in-Chief of the German navy, is third from the right. *Below:* Without the Liberty ship, Britain would have starved at some point in 1942 as the German submariners enjoyed their 'Happy Time'.

Above: An Atlantic convoy in 1941. *Below:* There were no grounds for complacency in the continuing battle against the U-boat threat, as reflected in this contemporary cartoon.

Although the Battle of Britain was over by 1941, the air raids still continued as part of a war of attrition. *Above:* London businesses bombed out of their premises left notices of their change of address on railings in the vicinity. *Below:* Damage at a London hospital and, right, French sailors help with the clear up following a night raid on Portsmouth on 10 January.

FEBRUARY 1941

Fires burn in the distance, marking the position of Tobruk. British infantrymen watch the billowing smoke as they await the order to advance on the Italian-held stronghold. By 16 January 1941 the Australian 6th Division had led the attack to capture the port of Bardia, taking around 70,000 Italians prisoner. Tobruk fell to the British and Australian forces on 22 January, and, further west along the coast, the port of Benghazi fell into their hands soon afterwards.

Although Operation Sealion, Germany's plan to invade Britain, had been postponed indefinitely in the autumn of 1940, the British could not drop their guard for a moment. As shown above, the army continued its training and these soldiers are carrying out execises in defending against enemy landing forces, and also practicing street fighting with a Bren gun in a village street.

While fighting continued in Libya, Britain remained strongly garrisoned against invasion. *Above:* General Sir John Dill, Chief of the Imperial General Staff, inspects men of the Western Command. *Below:* Six-inch howitzers on the move. Columns of motorised transport became a familar sight on otherwise peaceful country roads as the army continued its training.

Britain became the refuge for many soldiers and refugees from the German-occupied countries. *Top left:* A Norwegian gunner serving with the Royal Navy. *Top right:* Dutch soldiers in training. The lower photograph shows Dr Benes, the President of Czechoslovakia, accompanied by General Sikorski, the Prime Minister of Poland, inspecting Czech troops.

This page: Re-armed and equipped with British battle-dress, these soldiers of the Dutch Army are engaged in bayonet and shooting practice.

Above: The crew of a Bofors gun give a demonstration to the Prime Minister, Winston Churchill, who is accompanied by General de Gaulle, commander of the Free French forces, and also by General Sikorski. After the display by British armoured units they inspect the troops, below.

Wrecked churches became the staple diet of the British propagandists. 'The hand of the vandal shows itself again. Here is another well-known London church blasted by the night bomber.'

Guy's Hospital bombed. 'True to tradition, Nazi airmen continue to attack hospitals in their night assaults on London. Guy's Hospital is shown after enemy bombardment, and nurses pause to look at the wreckage as they salvage equipment from damaged wards.'

Above: Damage to the Parish Clerks' Company Hall in Wood Street in the City of London, on the right, and curates clear the debris in another Blitzed church. *Below:* Considerable damage was also caused in many of London's working-class districts during the night of 13 February.

Above: Infantrymen with fixed bayonets in mopping-up operations at the fall of Bardia, the Libyan port on the Mediterranean coast. *Below:* The fall of Bardia resulted in the capture of thousands of Italian prisoners and vast quantities of machine guns and rifles.

Above: Artillery in action during the advance on Tobruk. *Below:* Passing over one of the few bridges into Derna, left intact by the Italians.

Above: A little surprise, in the form of a booby trap, left by the Italians when they were driven out of Tobruk in Libya. *Below:* An Italian aircraft which had crashed into buildings during the fighting around Tobruk.

Another Italian wreck in the Libyan desert. This is a Fiat CR.42 Falco, 'Falcon', fighter biplane which had attempted to land with one of its wheels shot away. The CR.42 was the most widely produced Italian aircraft of the war – over 1,800 were built – and it also served with the Hungarian Air Force on the Eastern Front.

Above: An official photograph taken after the capture of Benghazi by the Australian 6th Division on 6 February. (It was later recaptured by Rommel's forces and changed hands several times during the course of the North Africa campaign.) An Italian destroyer, attacked by RAF aircraft, lies half submerged in the harbour. *Below:* A British sentry on guard at the harbourside at Benghazi.

More inspections. This time it is Lord Cranborne, Secretary of the Dominions, visiting a group of Newfoundland troops stationed in England. In the lower photograph he is shown a howitzer concealed under camouflage netting.

Above: With the camouflage netting now removed, the Newfoundland soldiers make the howitzer ready for action as Lord Cranborne looks on.

Left: On the Canadian east coast members of an anti-aircraft battery maintain their vigil of the sky using highly sensitive sound detection equipment and also with binoculars. They are on the look-out for marauding enemy aircraft.

Large numbers of German prisoners of war, mostly Luftwaffe aircrew, were shipped to internment camps in Canada, where it was felt they couldn't do much harm as they had little prospect of escaping and returning to the action.

Above: The King takes a ride in a Bren Gun Carrier during a visit to a Canadian unit stationed with Southern Command. Also known as a Universal Carrier, this lightly armoured vehicle had entered service before the war and was built in vast numbers by Vickers and other companies. As often happened on these official visits, the King was accompanied by his wife, shown below.

MARCH 1941

The formal agreement by which Britain leased Atlantic bases to the USA was signed in London on 27 March 1941. Winston Churchill, the Prime Minister, is adding his signature, watched by J. G. Winant, the US Ambassador, on the left, and Vincent Massey, the Canadian High Commissioner, right.

Above: The Minister of Labour, Ernest Bevin, led the call for the mobilisation of the workforce in March 1941 when he outlined the terms of the Essential Work Order. This called upon women, as well as those men deemed unfit to fight, to offer their services in the nation's hour of need.

Women of Britain – Come into the Factories

On 10 March 1941, Ernest Bevin, the Minister of Labour, announced plans for the full use of man- and woman-power. 'In fighting a war of this character, the proper use of man and woman-power is absolutely vital. The Forces, Civil Defence Services, production departments and Industry, all make their claims upon the Ministry of Labour and national Service to supply them with their requirements. First we have to obtain this labour power and then distribute it so that it might produce the most effective results...'

In a speech given in Necastle on the day after his broadcast, Bevin called for 100,000 women to sign up for munitions work within the next fortnight. They were not to wait for instruction or registration, but simply to come forward voluntarily. The Ministry also paid attention to the welfare of the women and their families. Plans were put in place to provide subsidised child care, and instructions were issued for management in those companies not used to employing women.

It wasn't only about the female workforce and Bevin wanted men in low medical grades, who were unsuited for military service, to also come forward for work in the munitions industry.

Top left: ATS volunteers working with the artillery, noting the position of anti-aircraft bursts with the aid of a graph-etched mirror. *Top right:* Making the cloth to make uniforms at a Ministry of Supply factory. *Bottom:* A training centre in East Ham where a new group of volunteers is receiving instruction in engineering practices in preparation for war work.

Opposite page: A highly romanticised view of an American tanker. *Above:* Riveters assemble an M3 Medium Tank at the Detroit Tank Arsenal.

The Arsenal of Democracy – 'Keep 'Em Fighting!'

At the outbreak of the war in 1939, the American military had only a small force of around 400 light tanks, consisting of the M1 Combat Car, later renamed as the Light Tank M1A2, and the Light Tank M2. Both of these were only equipped with machine guns originally, although the M2 was eventually beefed up with a 37-mm anti-tank gun. Developed in 1935 for the infantry branch of the US Army, the M2 featured a main gun turret plus a side turret, an arrangement that earned it the nickname 'Mae West'. Next came the Light Tank M3, which entered service in 1941 and featured a 37-mm gun in a small top turret. This vehicle should not be confused with the Medium Tank M3, which also had the 37-mm gun on a top turret together with a larger calibre 75-mm gun mounted in a distinctive offset sponson on one side of the hull. These were both supplied to the British and Soviet armies and it was the British who instigated the practice of naming US tanks after generals from the American Civil War. Thus the Medium Tank M3 became more famously known as the General Lee, or in a later version as the General Grant, although the 'General' was soon dropped and they became M3 Lee or M3 Grant.

The M3 served the British well in the North African campaign although there were drawbacks. The top turret gave it a very high profile and the side sponson restricted the arc of fire for the main gun. It was against this background that in April 1941 the Armored Force Board selected a design submitted by the Ordnance Department for a new medium tank. Known as the T6 initially, this featured a modified M3 chassis with a sloping hull and a fully rotating cast turret to house the M3 Lee's 75-mm gun. This became the M4, or Sherman tank. The first production model of the Sherman rolled off the lines of the Lima Locomotive Works in Ohio in February 1942. Insufficient casting facilities meant that a slab-sided welded-hull version was also developed.

In early 1941, the newly elected President Roosevelt had signed the Lend-Lease bill that neatly circumvented the neutrality legislation that prevented the sale of arms to belligerent nations. Roosevelt would call for the delivery of 45,000 of the new tanks in 1942 alone and production was spread between several main centres. The largest of these was the Detroit Tank Arsenal built by Chrysler alongside its car plant at Warren, a suburb of Detroit, Michigan. This produced the Medium Tank M3 and from June 1942 it also turned out the new M4s. At the peak of production the Detroit Tank Arsenal employed close to 25,000 workers, plus thousands more at sub-contractors scattered around the country. This workforce

Below: M3 Medium Tank. The Sherman would be built on a modified version of its chassis.

Above: The unmistakable wedge-like profile of the Sherman tank. This welded hull version was the M4A1, and these were the first of the Lend-Lease Shermans supplied to the British.

consisted of men for the most part and, taking a lead from the British, an increasing number of women. Enter Rosie the Riveter, represented on posters as the muscle-flexing, no-nonsense worker published by the War Production Committee. In fact Rosie was an aircraft riveter but her 'We Can Do It!' attitude came to epitomise the determination of the 6 million women who took on vital war work, often working forty-eight hours a week so that the men could be released for other duties. The American public also did their bit to support the war effort by buying War Bonds, raising the money to 'Keep 'Em Fighting'.

From 1941 to 1945 America's industrial might produced 40 per cent of the entire output of armaments among the combatant nations. It was a prodigious achievement that accounted for over 250,000 aircraft, 350 destroyers, nearly 600 Liberty ships, 200 submarines and almost 90,000 tanks. Of these around two-thirds were M4 Shermans or derivatives. And while the Shermans were no match for the German Panzers, especially the heavy tanks such as the Tiger I and II and the Panther, they outnumbered the Germans by a factor of ten-to-one. In many respects the Sherman was an inferior design, but with Rosie's help the Allies couldn't fail to win this numbers game.

Above: M3 Medium Tank in action on the proving ground. Its high profile made it vulnerable. *Below:* British Mk V Covenanters. Produced from 1939 to replace the Mk IV Cruiser, there were design problems, particularly with over-heating, and it was deemed unfit for service overseas.

British tanks. *Top:* Cruisers under production. *Bottom:* These are Valentine infantry tanks. Developed by Vickers, more than 8,000 Valentines were built during the war. They were supplied in large numbers to Russia, and also built under licence in Canada.

In the spring of 1941 the Luftwaffe resumed its bombing raids on targets within Britain. This dramatic image taken from a German publication shows a Heinkel He 111 bomber apparently attacking barrage balloons. In fact the Germans had learnt very early on that it was pointless attacking the balloons because, although vulnerable, they would be replaced in a matter of hours. Neither did the tethered balloons carry identification roundel markings.

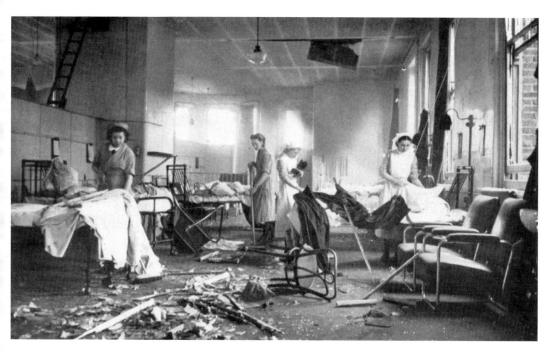

Above: The result of the night raid on London on 19 March 1941, one of the heaviest so far that year. According to the British press the Nazi bombs had an uncanny ability to fall on hospitals. *Below:* ATS drivers organised into parties to salvage bedding and linen from the rubble.

Top: Bombs dropped on London on 15 March struck a hall where a dance was in progress, and overturned a crowded bus. Several people were killed. *Bottom:* The bombs were indiscriminate and Buckingham Palace was hit on several occasions. This photograph shows damage caused to the North Lodge. A policeman on duty at the time was killed.

Opposite page: Children watch the aerial drama from the relative safety of a slit trench.

Above: It wasn't only in London that the Luftwaffe struck. This is the interior of the Roman Catholic Cathedral of St David, in Cardiff, the interior gutted by fire bombs.

Left: The Temple area in the City of London, with the Crown Office ripped open by the blasts. This is the centre for London's historic courts.

Opposite: The City of London would never be quite the same. In the upper photograph the tottering ruins are being made safe. The caption for the *Punch* cartoon: 'Actually this is now very much as Wren intended us to see St Paul's.'

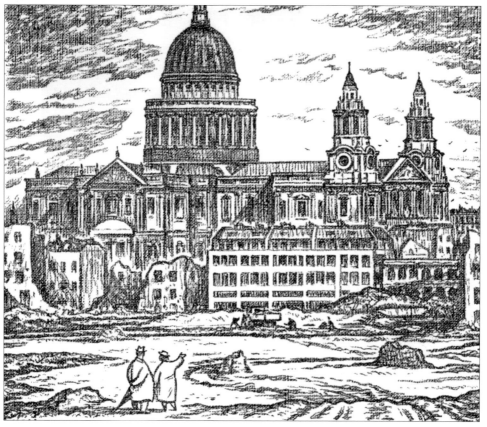

Above: A sixty-eight-year-old Liverpool grandmother sits with her daughter and grandchildren amid the ruins of their home. *Below:* The wreck of a Junkers Ju 88 bomber which crashed on this unidentified beach on the South Coast.

Above: Policemen guard the wreckage of a downed German aircraft. It was important to keep souvenir hunters away as the wreck might contain new equipment that needed to be examined. It would almost certainly contain potentially dangerous munitions. *Below:* These German airmen look happy enough to have arrived in London. For them the war really is over.

Above: Retrieving letters from a pillarbox which had been buried by debris in Paternoster Square, near St Paul's. Mail held up in this fashion would be inscribed as 'Delayed by Enemy Action'. *Below:* Churchill acknowledges the cheers of workmen in a bombed-out area of Manchester.

Above: Geoffrey Lloyd, Secretary for Mines, inspects gas producer equipment which had been adapted to power one of the London Fire Brigade's vehicles.

Running on Gas

In addition to the rationing of petrol, which had to be imported into the country, several measures were taken to find alternative forms of fuel to power vehicles for the essential services. The gas producers, such as the example shown above, burned wood in the form of charcoal, or sometimes coke, to generate enough gas to run the vehicle. But they were not popular as they could take up to fifteen minutes to be readied for a journey, they needed to be topped up, and the fumes were noxious. The gas producers were only suitable for petrol-driven vehicles – diesel engines would not work with the gas – and they generally produced less power and had a range limited to around 80 miles.

An alternative was to run the vehicle on town gas, which was readily available but had to be carried in large bags on the roof of the vehicles – a method previously used in the First World War. This was tried with some of the buses in London and in several major towns and cities, and this system was even adopted for some smaller vehicles and cars. However, the gas bags were bulky and there was the ever-present risk of fire, not to mention the danger of low bridges.

Above: A Food Flying Squad tanker being shown to the queen at Buckingham Palace. *Below:* A mobile canteen operated by the Women's Voluntary Service. The Dowager Marchioness of Reading is shown receiving the keys from the Nawab of Bahawalpur.

APRIL 1941

General List, the German commander in the Balkans, shown raising his baton to a column of his troops. With the exception of Greece, the Balkan nations were allies of Germany.

The Desert Fox and the Deutsche Afrika Korps

Under personal orders from Adolf Hitler, the Deutsche Afrika Korps was founded on 11 January 1941. A month later, on 12 February, one of the rising stars of the Blitzkrieg, Erwin Rommel, was put in command of the newly formed force. The Afrika Korps, as it became known, was formed to counter the dismal performance of the Italian troops in their African colonies. Between March and April 1941, the cobbled-together first troops of the Afrika Korps arrived in Libya to bolster the Italians already there. With Erwin Rommel in charge, they made some spectacular wins in the desert. They also made some severe losses too. The Western Desert campaign was, for the Germans, a sideshow to Russia, but for the British and their allies, it was, after the loss of Greece, the Balkans and Crete, the one sector where the British war effort could be concentrated. From 1940 until 1943, the Western Desert, from Egypt into Libya, was hard fought over. The hard rocky desert offered little in the way of cover, nor of shelter and temperatures varied from roasting to almost freezing, often within 24 hours.

The Afrika Korps, as a side show, was starved of the resources required for an all out victory and its ultimate defeat came about due to the lack of a protected, guaranteed supply chain and lack of supplies, which all had to be

Left: On 6 February 1941, Erwin Rommel was appointed commander of the new Deutsches Afrika Korps (DAK). His exploits in North Africa earned him the nickname of the 'Desert Fox'.

Above: Field-Marshal Rommel inspects men of the Deutsches Afrika Korps.

brought in from Italy by ship or by aircraft. Both were vulnerable to the British and many submarines operating from Gibraltar and Malta finished off ships destined to supply the Germans with much needed food and fuel.

The Afrika Korps had been sent to North Africa to ensure the Italians did not collapse under the pressure of the Allies and three times they attacked the Allies over the period from March 1941 until 1943, when they surrendered. Rommel launched his first offensive on 24 March 1941 and quickly took El Agheila and pushed the British back to Sollum on the Egypt–Libya border. All of Libya was recaptured apart from the port of Tobruk, which was besieged. The British held the Axis forces at the border and, with the Allies also holding Tobruk, which was strategically important, they effectively held control of the Suez Canal and the oil-rich lands beyond in the Middle East.

On 15 May 1941, the British made a limited offensive, recapturing Sollum and the Halfaya Pass, but Rommel attacked and the ground taken was lost again. A convoy from Gibraltar, loaded with tanks and aircraft, was sent to help the Allies, who again counter-attacked in November 1941 during Operation Crusader. The Siege of Tobruk was relieved and Rommel was forced to withdraw beyond El Agheila. Rommel was soon reinforced after several convoys with troops, tanks, fuel and other supplies were delivered and he attacked on 21 January 1942, forcing the British to retreat. By June 1942, the front line was west of Tobruk. Both sides spent the spring building up supplies and Rommel was first to attack. The Allies were defeated at Gazala and were soon in retreat. Tobruk was lost and the Germans did not stop until they reached El Alamein, where they were successfully stopped. It was a mere 70 miles to Alexandria. Soon Lieutenant-General Bernard Montgomery was in charge of the British forces and, in October 1942, he attacked at El Alamein again, winning the battle and pushing the Axis forces back. Many Italians were captured but the German tanks escaped. Tobruk was retaken on 13 November 1942 and the Germans pushed back further into Tunisia. With Tripoli lost to the Allies in January 1943, Rommel had huge supply problems and was forced further back, fighting rearguard actions along the way. They then had to fight against the Allied landings in Tunisia too, with the British 8th and 1st Armies sandwiching the Germans between them. On 13 May 1943, it was all over and the Germans surrendered in North Africa, after a series of battles between them and the British and Americans saw their numbers decline. With a lack of supplies due to Allied command of the air and sea, it was only a matter of time before they would have to surrender. Rommel himself was sent back to Germany before the fall and was sent to France to take control of defences there. We shall encounter him again in 1943 and 1944 when he bolsters the Atlantic Wall in readiness for the invasion of France by the Allies.

WH-683309

Left: An armoured car kicks up a cloud of dust in the African desert. The heat and dust were a constant problem in keeping machinery, such as the Messerschmitt Bf 110, shown opposite, in good running order. There were also issues in maintaining the supply chain – note the drums of petrol in the background.

On 20 and 21 March Plymouth suffered heavy raids, with high-explosive and incendiary bombs raining down. *Top:* People who have lost their homes stack their possessions in the street. *Bottom:* A soldier stands beside a wrecked house in Plymouth, its contents tumbling down.

Much of the damage caused by the raids on London was the result of incendiary bombs. *Above:* Two scenes at the height of the raids on 16 April 1941. Firemen fight to prevent the blaze from spreading. *Below:* Fires rage in central London. 'Lit by the torch of hate', as one report put it.

Men of the Auxiliary Fire Service playing water on a burning building in London, above. 'The Battle of the Flames is now the biggest job on the Home Front, and we have got to win it.' So said Herbert Morrison in a radio appeal for more volunteers to join the AFS. *Below*: A canvas water reservoir set up in a London street. A fire pump is attached to a taxi, on the right.

On the Thames at Westminster, the London Fire Brigade and AFS give a display during the London War Weapons Week held in May 1941.

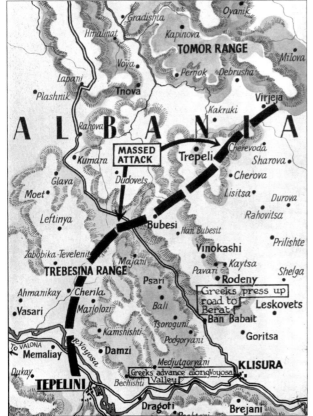

Above: A victory parade held in Athens. Field-Marshal List, seen holding the baton, led the German forces in the Greek campaign.

On 27 April 1941 the Allies evacuated their forces from Greece as the German Panzers rolled into the Greek capital. The Greek army had surrendered to the Germans and Italians four days earlier on 23 April. The Yugoslav government had signed its act of surrender on the 17th.

Left: For the Greeks, surrendering to the Italian forces had been especially humiliating as they had beaten them time and again over the previous months. This map shows Mussolini's battle-front stretching from Tepelini in the south to the Tomor Range in the north.

Above: British and Empire troops crowd the quayside in Crete after being landed from Greece, where thousands had taken part in the rearguard action to hold back the Axis forces. 'Close-up of a group of happy warriors recently returned from Greece. They look none the worse for their experience and smile cheerfully at the cameraman in proof of their undiminished spirit.'

Above: Following the night raids of 16 April two young Luftwaffe crewmen are shown at a London station on their way to an internment camp. *Below:* The remains of a German bomber brought down in the Kensington area during the raid.

MAY 1941

HMS *Hood* photographed before in Singapore before the war. On 23 May 1941, the German ships *Bismarck* and *Prinz Eugen* were located by the County-class cruisers *Norfolk* and *Suffolk* in the Denmark Strait between Iceland and Greenland. Being trailed by HMS *Hood* and HMS *Prince of Wales*, *Bismarck* destroyed the *Hood*, with the loss of almost all her crew, while severely damaging the *Prince of Wales*.

On 10 May 1941 the British authorities were stunned when Rudolf Hess, Hitler's deputy, flew to Scotland. Hess had flown the Messerschmitt Bf 110 from Germany on a mission to see the Duke of Hamilton in order to broker a peace agreement between Germany and Britain.

Above: The wreck of the aircraft, near Dungeval House, the duke's home. Nearly out of fuel, Hess had bailed out and landed by parachute.

Left: Hess's flight from Germany was a bitter personal blow for Adolf Hitler who described his deputy as suffering from hallucinations. Tried at Nuremburg after the war, Hess, who by then was the senior surviving Nazi following the suicide of Herman Goring, was sentenced to life imprisonment. He died at the Spandau prison in Berlin 1987 at the age of ninety-three. By that time he was the prison's only inmate.

Happy birthday to the Home Guard. *Above:* In honour of its first birthday on 14 May 1941, the Home Guard was invited to mount guard at Buckingham Palace for the day. The King is shown inspecting some of the men. At the height of its strength the Home Guard had around 1,500,000 men organised in 12,000 battalions.

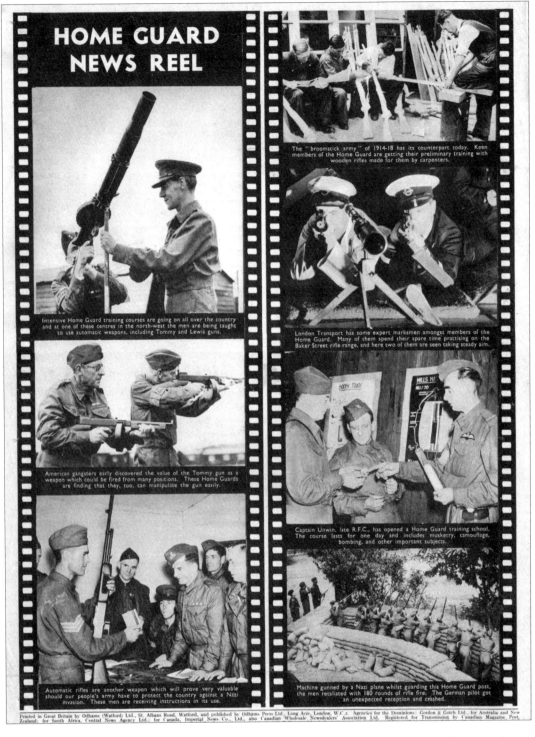

Although the imminent threat of invasion had largely subsided by 1941, the Home Guard continued to fulfill its duties until it was formally stood down in December 1944.

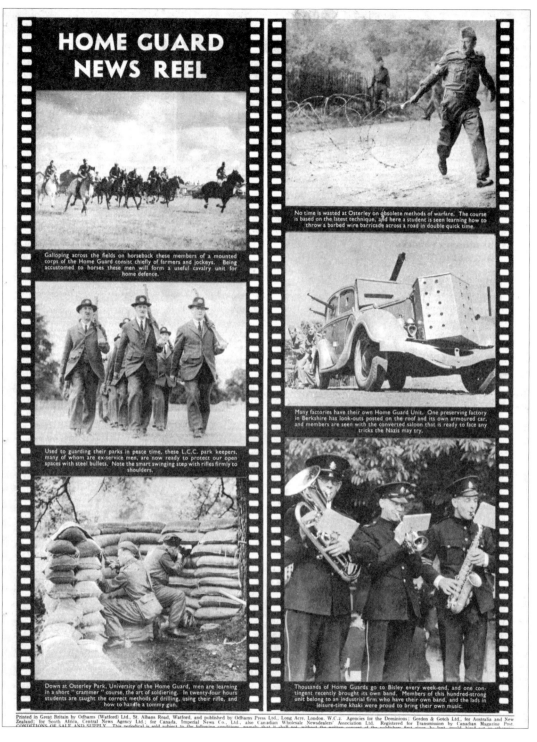

HOME GUARD NEWS REEL

Galloping across the fields on horseback these members of a mounted corps of the Home Guard consist chiefly of farmers and jockeys. Being accustomed to horses these men will form a useful cavalry unit for home defence.

Used to guarding their parks in peace time, these L.C.C. park keepers, many of whom are ex-service men, are now ready to protect our open spaces with steel bullets. Note the smart swinging step with rifles firmly to shoulders.

Down at Osterley Park, University of the Home Guard, men are learning in a short "crammer" course, the art of soldiering. In twenty-four hours students are taught the correct methods of drilling, using their rifle, and how to handle a tommy gun.

No time is wasted at Osterley on obsolete methods of warfare. The course is based on the latest technique, and here a student is seen learning how to throw a barbed wire barricade across a road in double quick time.

Many factories have their own Home Guard Unit. One preserving factory in Berkshire has look-outs posted on the roof and its own armoured car, and members are seen with the converted saloon that is ready to face any tricks the Nazis may try.

Thousands of Home Guards go to Bisley every week-end, and one contingent recently brought its own band. Members of this hundred-strong unit belong to an industrial firm who have their own band, and the lads in leisure-time khaki were proud to bring their own music.

Printed in Great Britain by Odhams (Watford) Ltd., St. Albans Road, Watford, and published by Odhams Press Ltd., Long Acre, London, W.C.2. Agencies for the Dominions: Gordon & Gotch Ltd., for Australia and New Zealand; for South Africa, Central News Agency Ltd.; for Canada, Imperial News Co., Ltd., also Canadian Wholesale Newsdealers' Association Ltd. Registered for Transmission by Canadian Magazine Post. CONDITIONS OF SALE AND SUPPLY. This periodical is sold subject to the following conditions, namely, that it shall not, without the written consent of the publishers first given, be lent, re-sold, hired

These 'News Reel' pages come from wartime editions of *Modern World*, a weekly publication that offered a pictorial review of news events at a halfpenny less than the *Picture Post*.

HMS *Dorsetshire* picking up surviviors from the *Bismarck* on 27 May 1941.

Above: British lorries blazing the way into Abyssinia for the convoys and troops to follow. The first battalion of Ethiopian troops to re-enter the country were led by an Australian officer. *Below:* Some of the Ethiopian troops armed and trained by the British to harass their Italian oppressors. They are photographed resting in a dried river-bed on their march into Abyssinia.

Above: An Italian aircraft brought down by the South African Air Force at Gobwen, Italian Somaliland, in present day Somalia. *Below:* The final stage of Emperor Haile Selassie's return to Abyssinia, on 5 May 1941, where he took command of Patriot Troops.

Above: Another view of the lorries making their way into Abyssinia. Thousands of camels loaded with stores and ammunition followed. The journey was made through 200 miles of jungle. The Italians now had to face a revolt backed by the British.

Above: Indian troops played a prominent part in the operations against the Italians in the campaign to capture Eritrea. They are shown here making their way across mountainous countryside. *Below:* At a forward position in Kenya, officers observe the return of an armoured car which had been on patrol in an area held by the Italians.

Above: South African troops presenting arms to the garrison at Fort Toseli on 19 May 1941. Around 18,000 prisoners were taken in the fighting in the Amba Alagi area. *Below:* Italian soldiers taken captive by the victorious South Africans at Mega.

Above: German paratroopers board a Ju 52 during training. The airborne troops had played a key role in the invasion of Norway and Denmark, and they hoped to repeat this in Crete.

The Invasion of Crete

In May 1941, an armada of Junkers Ju 52 transport aircraft dropped an airborne army of paratroops to spearhead the German invasion of the Greek island of Crete. This was to be a far bigger assault than the invasion of Denmark and Norway the previous year, and for the Luftwaffe's commanders Crete represented an opportunity to regain some prestige following the disastrous outcome of the Battle of Britain. The paratroops were to capture key points, including airfields which could be used to maintain the flow of supplies. However, the Allies were already aware of the imminent invasion through the interception of Ultra-coded messages, and the German forces encountered widespread fierce resistance from the island's population in addition to a large contingent of British and Commonwealth troops. In retaliation against the high level of casualties the Germans responded with extreme brutality, and more than 500 civilians were killed, their villages torched and the crops destroyed.

Above: The Ju 52 transport aircraft, which played a vital part in the invasion of Crete, receive a final overhaul as a prelude to action. *Below:* The parachutists prepare for the assault on the island on 22 May 1941. When they landed on Crete they were hampered by the method of dropping their weapons in individual cannisters and by the poor steering characteristics of their chutes. Consequently, many were left only lightly armed in the crucial period after landing.

A selection of poster art from a number of the Allied countries, termed the 'United Nations', including examples from France, the Netherlands, the Soviet Union, Mexico, Czechoslovakia, Canada, China and the USA.

Above and left: Building ships for the Merchant Navy. With the rate of attrition caused by the sinking of ships by the Germans and Italians, more ships had to be built and Britain's shipyards could not cope. Ship repair was necessary too, to make good the damage inflicted on ships which did make it safely to port. These two views show a cargo ship being built in a North East shipyard. By the year's end, the first Liberty Ships would be coming out of American shipyards in ever-increasing numbers.

THE RISKS
THEY RUN
FOR YOU

BOMB

SHELL

TORPEDO

MINE

Under the 'RED DUSTER'
they sustain our Island Fortress

Nearly one third of the world's Merchant Ships fly the RED ENSIGN

Above: Under the 'Red Duster'. By the nature of their jobs, seamen whose vessels were sunk lost wages from the time they abandoned ship. *Below:* A US Navy Lend-Lease destroyer on convoy escort duty.

Top: A British ship, safely launched, is towed from the river to the fitting out basin in a North East river. *Bottom:* Liberty Ship *Jeremiah O'Brien* is one of two Liberty Ships still afloat and is now a seagoing museum of the merchant marine in the Second World War.

The attack on Pearl Harbor. *Above:* USS *West Viginia* on fire, oil from her ruptured tanks spreading on the water. *Below:* Men from the US Naval Station of Manoche are placing Hawaiian garlands on the graves of comrades killed in the attack.

By late 1941 the scars caused by the night bombing raids on London were beginning to heal, revealing a new landscape from which the city would grow anew. This is the view from St Paul's Cathedral looking towards the Central Criminal Courts and Paternoster Square.

In the autumn of 1941 an exhibition by firemen artists was held at the Royal Academy on the theme of London's ordeal by fire. 'These painters, who were also the defenders of London, expressed the grim drama in which they were the principal participants with stark realism.'

Right: 'Smouldering Ruins of St Andrew's, Holborn', painted by Bernard Hailstone.

Below: 'Hose Laying', by E. G. Turner.

Above: Begining in June 1941, the RAF's fighters began daylight sweeps over the Channel and Occupied France to attack enemy aircraft and ground facilities. This photograph shows a formation of Hurricanes heading out towards the Channel. *Below:* Vickers-Armstrong Wellington bombers setting out on a daylight raid against industrial targets in Germany. The first of these operations was carried out on 12 April 1941.

Above: A Junkers Ju 87 Stuka dive-bomber on an airfield in Sicily with Mount Etna in the background. The Germans used the island as a base from which to attack Malta and Allied shipping in the Mediterranean. *Below*: A large Reihenbild Rb 30 camera being loaded on a Messerschmitt Bf 110 reconnaissance aircraft operating in the North African desert

Above: German and Italian soldiers on guard at the gates of Bardia, the Mediterranean seaport in eastern Libya. The Battle of Bardia was fought over three days between 3 and 5 January 1941 as part of the Allies' Western Desert Campaign. *Below:* A German guard outside the ancient temple of Apollonia on the Balkan Peninsula.

In May 1941 German paratroops led the airborne assault against the Greek island of Crete. Their role was to capture key points, including airfields which could be used to maintain the supply chain. However the Allies were aware of the imminent invasion through the interception of coded messages, and the German invaders encountered widespread fierce resistance.

Right: A German paratrooper. Note the stick-grenade.

Below: The paratroops relax after heavy fighting on Crete.

Above: In the 'House of German Art'. An image from the Great German Art Exhibition held in Munich. This idealised image, painted by Franz Eichhorst, is entitled 'Soldier in Poland'.

Three scenes showing the German advance into Russia. *Above:* Burning houses, have been set alight by the retreating Soviet forces as part of Stalin's rigorous scorched earth policy. *Below left:* Pity the poor infantryman who was expected to march for as much as 40 miles a day in the relentless push eastwards. *Below right:* Combing through a field of maize.

German mounted troops on the Eastern Front. Originally published in the *Signal* propaganda magazine, the caption for this photograph stated: 'The great battle of Bialystok and Minsk has been brought to a victorious conclusion – the cavalry vanguards of the German armies are now pushing far ahead of the infantry in pursuit of the enemy.'

Above: The view from a Fieseler Storch reconnaissance aircraft, looking down upon an advancing column of German troops on the Eastern Front.

Right: Another aircraft above the action, this time a twin-engined Messerschmitt Bf 110. 'The tank advance guard halts somewhere in the wide Caucasian steppes. The close-range reconnaissance plane transmits the enemy's position to them. The tanks immediately move forward against the enemy who is well hidden in the tall steppe grass.'

A Christmas cartoon from the *Punch* Almanack for 1941.

JUNE 1941

A German car equipped with loud speakers races through the Russian town of Smolensk, calling upon the inhabitants to surrender. The buildings are ablaze, set on fire by the retreating Russian forces as part of Stalin's scorched earth policy. The Germans captured the town on 16 July 1941.

Behind the scenes. *Above:* Radiolocation, or Radar as we know it nowadays, was Britain's secret defence against the German bombers. An RAF controller is shown at the control of a desk of a transmitting station. *Below:* The WAAF girls on the switchboard ensure that all communications are dealt with speedily in order to intercept the incoming bombers.

Above: WAAFs plot the movements of the German aircraft, following information provided by the radiolocation transmitters. *Below:* Inside an operating room of RAF Fighter Command, deep underground. Senior officers watch the movement of aircraft indicated on the map below.

The initial four main drives against Soviet forces: towards Leningrad in the north, another towards Moscow, the third in the direction of Kiev, and the fourth with Odessa as the objective.

Barbarossa – Ost Front

The Führer and Supreme Commander of the Armed Forces
Führer Headquarters, 18th December 1940. 9 copies

Directive No. 21 'Case Barbarossa'

The German Armed Forces must be prepared, even before the conclusion of the war against England, to crush Soviet Russia in a rapid campaign ('Case Barbarossa'). The Army will have to employ all available formations to this end, with the reservation that occupied territories must be insured against surprise attacks.
The Air Force will have to make available for this Eastern campaign supporting forces of such strength that the Army will be able to bring land operations to a speedy conclusion and that Eastern Germany will be as little damaged as possible by enemy air attack. This build-up of a focal point in the East will be limited only by the need to protect from air attack the whole combat and arsenal area which we control, and to ensure that attacks on England, and especially upon her imports, are not allowed to lapse.
The main efforts of the Navy will continue to be directed against England even during the Eastern campaign.

Below: A land laid waste. As the Soviets retreated they put the houses to the torch.

In certain circumstances I shall issue orders for the deployment against Soviet Russia eight weeks before the operation is timed to begin.

Preparations which require more time than this will be put in hand now, in so far as this has not already been done, and will be concluded by 15th May 1941.

It is of decisive importance that our intention to attack should not be known.

The preparations of the High Commands will be made on the following basis:

I. General Intention

The bulk of the Russian Army stationed in Western Russia will be destroyed by daring operations led by deeply penetrating armoured spearheads. Russian forces still capable of giving battle will be prevented from withdrawing into the depths of Russia.

The enemy will then be energetically pursued and a line will be reached from which the Russian Air Force can no longer attack German territory. The final objective of the operation is to erect a barrier against Asiatic Russia on the general line Volga–Archangel.

The last surviving industrial area of Russia in the Urals can then, if necessary be eliminated by the Air Force.

In the course of these operations the Russian Baltic Fleet will quickly lose its bases and will then no longer be capable of action.

The effective operation of the Russian Air Force is to be prevented from the beginning of the attack by powerful blows.

Below: Soviet Tupolev TB-3 heavy bombers in flight. First flown in 1930 the TB-3 looks out of date and it was obsolete by the outbreak of the war. Officially it was withdrawn in 1939, but many continued in operation throughout the war. Its main successor was the Petlyakov Pe-8, which was used to bomb Berlin in August 1941.

II. Probable Allies and Their Tasks

1. On the flanks of our operations we can count on the active support of Rumania and Finland in the war against Soviet Russia.

The High Command of the Armed Forces will decide and lay down in due time the manner in which the forces of these two countries will be brought under German command.

2. It will be the task of Rumania to support the attack of the German southern flank, at least at the outset, with its best troops ; to hold down the enemy where German forces are not engaged; and to provide auxiliary services in the rear areas.

3. Finland will cover the advance of the Northern Group of German forces moving from Norway (detachments of Group XXI) and will operate in conjunction with them. Finland will also be responsible for eliminating Hangö.

4. It is possible that Swedish railways and roads may be available for the movement of the German Northern Group, by the beginning of the operation at the latest.

III. Conduct of Operations

A. Army (in accordance with plans submitted to me): In the theatre of operations, which is divided by the Pripet Marshes into a Southern and a Northern sector, the main weight of attack will be delivered in the Northern area. Two Army Groups will be employed here.

The more southerly of these two Army Groups (in the centre of the whole front) will have the task of advancing with powerful armoured and motorised formations from the area about and north of Warsaw, and routing the enemy forces in White Russia. This will make it possible for strong mobile forces to advance northwards and, in conjunction with the Northern Army Group operating out of East Prussia in the general direction of Leningrad, to destroy the enemy forces operating in the Baltic area. Only after the fulfilment of this first essential task, which must include the occupation of Leningrad and Kronstadt, will the attack be continued with the intention of occupying Moscow, an important centre of communications and of the armaments industry.

Only a surprisingly rapid collapse of Russian resistance could justify the simultaneous pursuit of both objectives.

The most important task of Group XXI, even during these eastern operations, remains the protection of Norway. Any forces available after carrying out this task will be employed in the North (Mountain Corps), at first to protect the Petsamo area and its iron ore mines and the Arctic highway, then to advance with Finnish forces against the Murmansk railway and thus prevent the passage of supplies to Murmansk by land.

The question whether an operation of this kind can be carried out with stronger German forces (two or three divisions) from the Rovaniemi area and south of it will depend on the willingness of Sweden to make its railways available for troop transport.

It will be the duty of the main body of the Finnish Army, in conjunction with the advance of the German North flank, to hold down the strongest possible Russian

Some of the ten million. *Top:* Soviet troops marching during a display of strength in Moscow. *Bottom:* A look of determination and concentration on the faces of these young machine-gunners fighting in what would become known as 'The Great Patriotic War' against Germany.

forces by an attack to the West, or on both sides of Lake Ladoga, and to occupy Hangö.

The Army Group operating south of the Pripet Marshes will also seek, in a concentric operation with strong forces on either flank, to destroy all Russian forces west of the Dnieper in the Ukraine. The main attack will be carried out from the Lublin area in the general direction of Kiev, while forces in Rumania will carry out a wide enclosing movement across the lower Pruth. It will be the task of the Rumanian Army to hold down Russian forces in the intervening area.

When the battles north and south of the Pripet Marshes are ended the pursuit of the enemy will have the following aims:

In the South the early capture of the Donets Basin, important for war industry.

In the North a quick advance to Moscow. The capture of this city would represent a decisive political and economic success and would also bring about the capture of the most important railway junctions.

B. Air Force

It will be the duty of the Air Force to paralyse and eliminate the effectiveness of the Russian Air Force as far as possible. It will also support the main operations of the Army, i.e. those of the central Army Group and of the vital flank of the Southern Army Group. Russian railways will either be destroyed or, in accordance with operational requirements, captured at their most important points (river crossings) by the bold employment of parachute and airborne troops.

In order that we may concentrate all our strength against the enemy Air Force and for the immediate support of land operations, the Russian armaments industry will not be attacked during the main operations. Such attacks will be made only after the conclusion of mobile warfare, and they will be concentrated first on the Urals area.

C. Navy

It will be the duty of the Navy during the attack on Soviet Russia to protect our own coasts and to prevent the break-out of enemy naval units from the Baltic. As the Russian Baltic fleet will, with the capture of Leningrad, lose its last base and will then be in a hopeless position, major naval action will be avoided until this occurs.

After the elimination of the Russian fleet the duty of the Navy will be to protect the entire maritime traffic in the Baltic and the transport of supplies by sea to the Northern flank (clearing of minefields!).

IV.

All steps taken by Commanders-in-Chief on the basis of this directive must be phrased on the unambiguous assumption that they are precautionary measures undertaken in case Russia should alter its present attitude towards us. The number of officers employed on preliminary preparations will be kept as small as possible and further staffs will be designated as late as possible and only to the extent required for the duties of each individual. Otherwise there is a danger that

Tank on tank. *Above:* the Soviet T34 has been acclaimed as the most effective and influential tank of the Second World War with its balance of firepower, armour, mobility and ruggedness. Introduced into service in 1940, it became the mainstay of the Red Army's armoured forces and over 84,000 were built by the time production finally ceased in 1958. *Below:* In comparison, the German Panzer IV had served well in an infantry support role in the lightning-fast situation of the Blitzkrieg, but on the Eastern Front it more than met its match in the T34 despite an upgrade of its gun to 75 mm. Over 6,000 IVs would be lost in the fight against Russia.

premature knowledge of our preparations, whose execution cannot yet be timed with any certainty, might entail the gravest political and military disadvantages.

V.

I await submission of the plans of Commanders-in-Chief on the basis of this directive.

The preparations made by all branches of the Armed Forces, together with time-tables, are to be reported to me through the High Command of the Armed Forces.

Signed: ADOLF HITLER

It was this document that set in motion the ultimate downfall of the 1,000-year Reich. Designed to give the Germans the 'living space' they so craved, and to provide slave labour for their industry, it would also remove once and for all the threat from Soviet Russia. Operation Barbarossa was a campaign of superlatives. Some 4 million soldiers, the largest invasion force in history, would advance along a 2,000-mile front, using 600,000 vehicles and 625,000 horses, making it an invasion on a scale never seen before, nor likely to be seen again. Between 1941 and 1944, some 95 per cent of all German casualties were on the Eastern Front and it accounted for some 65 per cent of all Allied military casualties of the war. Russia bore the brunt of the fighting from 1941 to 1944 and saw its western provinces all but destroyed as a result of the fighting. The initial start date of 15 May 1941 was impossible to meet, not least because of the commitments in Yugoslavia and Greece, which delayed the start of Barbarossa until 22 June 1941. At the time, the start date did not seem important but by the winter of 1941/42, it was painfully obvious that the war had started too late.

Barbarossa was the biggest campaign of any war in history, saw the most casualties, the largest number of men and equipment captured (on both sides) and the biggest tank battles that will ever be. German fighter pilots were credited with hundreds of kills each and the Eastern Front campaign was the first total war, where both sides committed huge atrocities on an almost daily basis, and in the worst conditions imaginable. Some 3 million Russian soldiers were captured in 1941 and these were forced to work for the Germans and effectively starved to death as part of the plan to cut the population of Eastern Europe.

The campaign itself involved three German and Axis armies, Army Groups North, Centre and South, with each having clear objectives. As seen from the directive, the plan was to bypass Russian armies and encircle them and either kill or take prisoners the hundreds of thousands caught in these traps. At the time of the attack, Russia and Germany were at peace and with a non-aggression pact between themselves, which had split Eastern Europe into Russian and German spheres of influence, but Hitler had declared some fifteen years before of the need to attack and occupy swathes of Russia so as to provide food and supplies for the Germans. One of the major factors though was the oil in Azerbaijan. With their oil mainly coming from Romanian oil fields, the Germans needed more and the Baku oilfield was the obvious solution. This, and the relative prosperity of the Ukraine, with its industry and rich agricultural land, saw Army Group South as key to the campaign. The first target, however, was Leningrad, with the south second and Moscow a poor third. Ultimately, the Germans would be led into a war of attrition with the largest nation on earth, and like the Japanese a few months later, would commit an act of folly that would see their downfall. Despite a build-up taking months and a massing of German and Axis troops on the borders of Russia, beginning in February 1941, the Russians were caught by surprise. The Germans had undertaken subterfuge, including exercises and deception to give the impression Britain was the real objective. The Russians were even given the date of the start of Barbarossa by spies and the British, who had been breaking Ultra messages. The Soviets had industrialised in the 1930s and had an industrial output that could match Germany's and was only just below that of the pre-war USA. Russia was also sure a war with Germany would come but did not expect it until 1943, and was planning accordingly. Surprisingly, the Russians had some 23,000 tanks in service and this was unexpected by the Germans, who had just over 5,200.

The attack started at 0315 on Sunday 22 June 1941 and the next few months would be a series of Russian defeats. On the first day alone, with a loss of thirty-five aircraft, the Luftwaffe destroyed around 2,000 Soviet planes. Almost double that number were destroyed in the first three days, giving the Germans an opportunity to use their dive bombers to best effect. Much fighting took place in the south and centre of the Soviet Union, with encircling battles taking place at cities like Minsk and Smolensk, with the loss of sometimes hundreds of thousands of Russians. Within a month, the Germans realised they had underestimated the Russian strength and could not make further huge offensive gains until the supply chain caught up with the front line troops. Between August and October Kiev was encircled and captured, and troops reached the outskirts of Leningrad. Between October and the beginning of December, attempts were made for the final push on Moscow, which was heavily defended. The weather deteriorated and the onward advance was slowed hugely. No longer would heavy gains be made and by 2 December, despite the German 258th Infantry Division being within 15 miles of the centre of Moscow, the German troops managed another few miles before the winter stalled their progress. Ill-equipped for a winter campaign, conditions were atrocious. From a low of 90,000 men, now some half a million Soviet soldiers faced the freezing Wehrmacht troops. On 5 December, a Russian campaign started, which threw the Germans back almost 200 miles from Moscow. It was to be the beginning of the end for the Nazis. 210,000 were killed and 620,000 wounded. The winter would be harsh and the better prepared Russians kept up the pressure against the frozen, hungry and ill-equipped Axis troops. The Germans would attack again in the spring and take more Russian land but the campaign had seen so many deaths and injuries that the Germans were fatally injured as a result of the attacks of 1941 and the subsequent campaign in 1942. Like the forthcoming attack on Pearl Harbour, Operation Barbarossa was an initial success that awoke a slumbering giant that would ultimately triumph over the aggressor.

A woman factory worker in Moscow. In the war of attrition it was industrial power and not firepower that would decide the outcome.

Above: HMS *Auckland*, one of three Egret-class sloops launched in 1938, and shown here off Tobruk on 21 June 1941. Three days later she was attacked and sunk by a swarm of German Ju 87 Stuka dive-bombers near Tobruk.

The final moments of HMS *Auckland* after being attacked by German dive-bombers on 24 June 1941. Her crew was machine-gunned in the water as they abandoned ship.

A casualty of a British raid during the desert campaign, 1941.

Top: Soldiers of all types played their part in the campaign in Syria. Patrols of the border were maintained by the Transjordan Frontier Force, which included Arabs, Circassians, Sudanese and Egyptians. A mechanised squadron is shown on parade. The map shows the scene of the Allied advance in the Middle East.

JULY 1941

Gunnery practice for RAF bomber crews using an electric 'hare'. Mounted on a track, the hare-plane would run at high speed while the gunner worked the mobile turret.

During 1941 the RAF fighter pilots were taking the initiative with sorties across the Channel and into enemy territory. *Above:* A Spitfire pilot unloads his parachute after a mission.

Above: A Hurricane on patrol. For every aircraft in the air there was a dedicated back-up team on the ground. Shown below, these mechanics work on one of the engines of an Avro Anson. This was a multi-role twin-engined aircraft that served with many Commonwealth air forces.

The Bristol Beaufighter was a long-range twin-engined fighter derived from the earlier Beaufort design. Introduced in 1940, by early 1941 it had proved itself as an effective counter to the Luftwaffe's night bombers. It also went on to serve overseas.

American-built Boston bombers nearing completion.
1941 was also noteworthy as the year in which the
new Avro Lancaster four-engined heavy bomber
first took to the skies. The Lancaster would enter
service in 1942.

Above: RAF ground staff are shown 'bombing up' a Fairey Battle light bomber. Despite having the same Merlin engine as a Spitfire, the Battle was weighed down by its three-man crew and bombload, and its slow speed made it vulnerable. *Below:* Members of a Czechoslovak squadron head for their Wellington bomber for another raid into enemy territory.

Night-time acclimatisation for this bomber crew entails wearing dark glasses so that their eyes became accustomed to the conditions outside.

A fighter squadron's score-board with the tally of raids recorded on the blade of a German aircraft.

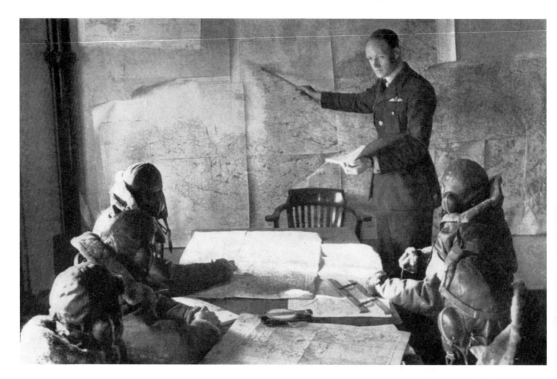

Co-operation of Army and the RAF became highly organised with the Westland Lysander engaged in important joint missions. The Lysander's excellent short take-off and landing characteristics made it the ideal aircraft for covert missions into occupied France. Here RAF pilots seconded to the Army Co-operation Command RAF are briefed before a training mission.

AUGUST 1941

A *poilu* – the old term for a French infantryman – taking a drink of water in the desert.
Established in London in June 1940, the Free French government-in-exile was led by Charles de
Gaulle and its soldiers fought on several battlefields from the Middle East to North Africa.

In August 1941, Winston Churchill and President Rossevelt took part in the Atlantic Conference, which took place on board HMS *Prince of Wales* off the Newfoundland coast. It resulted in the Atlantic Charter, a joint proclamation by the USA and Britain stating that they were fighting the Axis powers in order to 'ensure life, liberty, independence and religious freedom, and to preserve the rights of man and justice'.

Above: A British paratrooper home on leave asks a War Reserve Constable for directions. The WRC was a voluntary role introduced in 1939. Their duties including the usual policing activities, as well as enforcing the blackout, assisting in air-raid precautions and dealing with black marketeers and deserters.

Right: 'So polite aren't they. Really, I'm almost beginning to prefer these Utility policemen.'

Above: Operating in East Africa, an American-built Glen Martin Maryland A-22 light bomber and reconnaissance aircraft. *Below:* A bakery in the desert.

Above: British soldiers with their heads covered by netting as they sit beside a tank to write letters home. *Below:* Crew members of a British armoured car take Holy Communion in the heat of the desert.

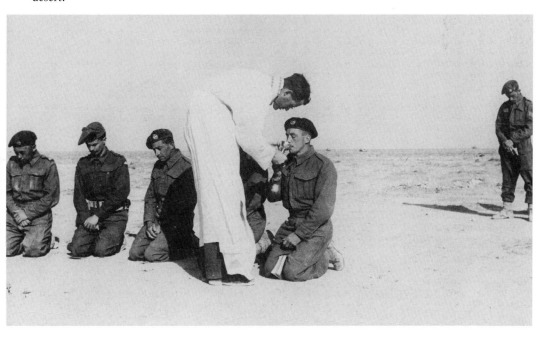

Top: British water-carts or bowsers taking on water at a filling point left behind by the Italians. Another method of distributing water to the forces using old petrol cans is shown in the bottom photograph.

SEPTEMBER 1941

If a picture paints a thousand words then a single well-observed cartoon can convey a million. By turning against his former ally, Hitler had woken the Russian bear that would prove his undoing on the Eastern Front.

By 8 September 1941 the German advance into Russia saw Leningrad encircled. These photographs from the Eastern Front were taken by photographers of the Propaganda Kompanie and published in *Signal*, the German propaganda magazine. In addition to being issued to the armed forces and the Home Front, *Signal* was produced in several languages and was made available throughout the Continent and in the USA.

Left: Summertime action in the East, with an infantryman photographed in front of a burning barn.

Below: Street fighting in the town of Zhitomir, about 80 miles from Kiev.

Top: German Panzer IV tanks on the move, 'somewhere in Russia'. *Bottom:* These portrait studies of the fighting men were typical fare for the PK's snappers. On the left is a mountain soldier with a long range-finder. 'Work with a range-finder in the Steppes of Russia is child's play for the mountain gunner, and his shots always hit their mark.' On the right, 'No. 1 gunner has gone through a special course of training and is an expert on indirect fire'.

Above: The mountains and glens of Scotland provided the setting for training anti-tank riflemen of
Scottish Command. *Below:* The Duke of Gloucester paid a visit to British troops in Northern Ireland.
They are showing how speedily a truck can be loaded with equipment.

Above: Hurricanes on patrol, flying in formation over Northern Ireland. *Below:* A maintenance crew overhauling one of the aircraft's Merlin engines at an RAF station in the province.

The Army and RAF collaborated in parachute training for the British paratroops. The jumps were made from the long-nosed Armstrong Whitworth AW38 Whitley, shown top. This was one of three twin-engine bombers in service with the RAF at the outbreak of the war. It was retired from frontline service in 1942.

Brewster Buffalo F2As being assembled in Malaya in late 1941. The US aircraft were bought by the British to make up for a shortfall in numbers. Designated as the Brewster Buffalo Mk 1 by the Brits, the aircraft of No. 243 Squadron took on the Japanese forces who invaded Malaya on 8 December 1941.

OCTOBER 1941

Fresh forces – a column of soldiers marches through a Russian city in 1941, on its way to fight against the Nazi invaders.

On Arctic patrols. These photographs show the freezing conditions encounted by the Royal Navy on their patrols in northern waters. The bridge, decks and guns are thickly coated with ice.

'Ice holds this warship in its grip, but she still goes about her duties. The navy's task is ceaseless, and officers and men accept the worst kind of weather as just part of the job.'

'At 35 degress below zero.' With the approach of winter on the Eastern Front the Germans were discovering that their greatest adversary was going to be the Russian winter conditions.

NOVEMBER 1941

HMS *Ark Royal* just before the start of the Second World War. By the 1930s, it had been realised by some that the aircraft carrier was the most important ship type in existence. It was not until the attack on Taranto in 1940 that its importance was obvious to all.

HMS *Ark Royal* after her launching at Cammell Laird's Birkenhead yard in 1937.

Some of her Fairey Swordfish aircraft fly over *Ark Royal*. Introduced in 1936, the Swordfish was a torpedo bomber, but its biplane design earned it the nickname 'Stringbag' and it was looking outmoded by the outbreak of war. Even so, it remained in production until 1944.

HMS *Ark Royal* – The Ship the Germans Sank More than Once

Designed in 1934, one of the most famous of aircraft carriers of the Second World War was HMS *Ark Royal*. Built at Birkenhead by Cammell Laird, the *Ark Royal* was 27,720 tons and 800 feet long. It was capable of carrying around sixty aircraft and took part in numerous campaigns, from the failed invasion and defence of Norway in 1940, spent much time in the Mediterranean in 1940–41, and was instrumental in the sinking of the *Bismarck* and of the Malta convoys of 1941. She was so famous that the Germans claimed her sunk on numerous occasions. *Ark Royal* had two hanger decks and came about as a result of the 1934 Navy building programme. The keel was laid in 1935 and the ship was launched in 1937, with fitting out taking until autumn 1938, and commissioning taking place on 16 December that year.

In September 1939, *Ark Royal* was used to hunt for submarines but the loss of HMS *Courageous* saw the end of this use for the vessel. *Ark Royal* had had a lucky escape on 14 September, when two torpedoes from U-39 passed close by. U-39, within the hour, became the first U-boat casualty of the war. On 25 September, another near miss by a Junkers Ju 88 saw a bomb nearly hit the carrier. The Germans claimed a kill, despite a total miss. *Ark Royal* was sent to West Africa to help in the hunt for the *Graf Spee* as part of Force K. She escorted Exeter back to Plymouth after the Battle of the River Plate and was sent to Scapa Flow before heading for the Mediterranean. She had reached Gibraltar when the news of the

Below: HMS *Glorious* was an older type of aircraft carrier, and originally converted from a First World War battleship. She had been sunk in 1940 off Norway.

invasion of Norway reached the ship and she turned around to head north. She was stationed off Norway to provide fighter cover for the British ships and troops. She was used in the evacuation of Narvik and searched for the *Scharnhorst* and *Gneisenau* after they had sunk the carrier *Glorious* and her destroyer escort.

With *Hood*, she was sent to the Mediterranean in mid-June and was involved in the attack on the Vichy French fleet at Mers-el-Kebir. By the end of 1940, *Ark Royal* was sent into the Atlantic to search for commerce raiders and in February 1941, she was sent to search for *Gneisenau* and *Scharnhorst* again. Damaged by a Swordfish's depth charges, the *Ark Royal* returned to Gibraltar for repair as the two German ships escaped. April 1941 was spent alternating between Atlantic sorties and aiding convoys to Malta, while, in May, she was used to defend a convoy heading for Alexandria and later in the month to send Hurricanes to Malta.

In mid-May, the *Bismarck* and *Prinz Eugen* had broken out into the Atlantic and sunk the *Hood*. *Ark Royal* was tasked to help locate her and destroy her and the hunt for the *Bismarck* was on. On 26 May, a Swordfish from the *Ark Royal* located *Bismarck* and the fleet began chase. Soon more were in the air and after a failed attempt, which saw some torpedoes head for HMS *Sheffield*, the Swordfish were rearmed and heading for the *Bismarck* once more. Three torpedoes hit the *Bismarck*, with one damaging her steering gear. The next day, British naval forces caught up with *Bismarck* and she was sunk.

Ark Royal returned to escorting Malta convoys and on 10 November 1941 was ferrying aircraft to Malta. Three days later, on the return to Gibraltar, at 1540, *Ark Royal* was hit amidships by a torpedo from U-81. The carrier was abandoned but her condition stabilised. She was reboarded and taken in tow but continued to flood and list heavily. Her crew of 1,487 were all safely taken off, and apart from one casualty during the initial hit, no one else was killed or injured. At 0619 on 14 November, *Ark Royal* split in two and sank. Hitler could finally claim she was sunk. In 2002, the wreck was rediscovered.

Opposite page:
Ark Royal being
escorted by HMS
Wren.

Right, top and middle:
These two views show
the reality of war. The
first shows the very
real threat of bombs as
four straddle the *Ark
Royal*, the other is a
propaganda postcard
issued in 1939. Many
of these near misses
were what led the
Germans to claim
they had sunk *Ark
Royal* on numerous
occasions.

Bottom right:
Ark Royal was finally
sunk off Gibraltar in
1941. This view shows
many of her crew
abandoning ship as the
aircraft carrier lists,
with no power.

November 1941 was the first anniversary of the first all-aircraft ship-to-ship attack when Royal Navy Swordfish took-off from HMS *Illustrious* to attack the Italian battle fleet at anchor in Taranto. The occasion was marked by the publication of these images of the Fleet Air Arm at work. *Top:* Below deck on an aircraft carrier with a Supermarine Walrus being wheeled out of the hangar. *Bottom:* Sailors wheeling bombs towards the waiting aircraft.

Above: A Walrus biplane taking off from the deck of a Royal Navy carrier. The man with the flag, on the left, gives the pilot the signal to go. The aircraft had been designed in the 1930s by Supermarine's R. J. Mitchell.

Right: Coastal patrols and convoy escorts were conducted by RAF Coastal Command. An air gunner/observer, complete with guns, pauses for the photographer on the way to his aircraft.

DECEMBER 1941

Above: A Japanese Mitsubishi Zero fighter about to take off for Pearl Harbor from the carrier *Akagi* on 7 December 1941.

Opposite page: A view from a Japanese bomber of the attack on Pearl Harbor, top. The attack came as a surprise to the soldiers and sailors at Pearl Harbor, although many expected the Japanese and Americans to go to war. The USS *West Virginia* ablaze, bottom, her colours still flying as she burns.

Above: USS *Shaw* ablaze. This was a Mahan-class destroyer commissioned in 1936. This view shows the explosion of her forward magazine at 0930 on 7 December. *Shaw* was in dry dock during the attack and caught fire after being hit by numerous bombs. *Shaw* was temporarily repaired at Pearl and sailed for San Francisco, where she was repaired fully. She survived the war and was scrapped in July 1946. *Below:* The remains of USS *Oklahoma*. She was completed in 1916 and was based at Pearl Harbor from 1937. On Battleship Row, she was hit by three torpedoes and started to capsize. Hit by two more torpedoes, her crew were strafed as they tried to escape the sinking ship. 429 were killed or missing as a result of the Japanese attack.

Pearl Harbor – Awakening the Sleeping Giant

Taranto, November 1940! The nighttime raid on this Italian naval base by around twenty Fairey Swordfish torpedo bombers flying from one aircraft carrier was carefully studied by the Japanese. Basically, the British Fleet Air Arm bombers dropped down unexpectedly on Taranto in one of the most daring raids of the war. With numerous battleships and cruisers in harbour, the use of torpedoes in shallow water was untested but proved to be successful. The Japanese naval attaché to Berlin went to Taranto to see the effects of the raid and reported back to Tokyo.

With economic sanctions on Japan and a ban on exporting oil to the country, the war-mongering factions pushed for a war with America. The Japanese knew the war would have to be short and the opportunities presented at Taranto showed them the way forward. A raid on the American navy's Pacific base of Pearl Harbor, on the island of Oahu, was the way forward. The plan was simple, using a fleet of six carriers to destroy the American aircraft carriers at their base, and to destroy the naval facilities at Pearl so as to make the base inoperable. The attack on Pearl wasn't the first on an American ship that day. A small freighter heading for Pearl Harbor, the *Cynthia Olson*, disappeared that day too, with the loss of thirty-five lives. Shadowed by a Japanese submarine, the I-26, she was torpedoed that morning some 300 miles off the coast of California, and was the first ship sunk by a Japanese submarine during the war. Her loss was overshadowed by the much more major event unfolding in Hawaii.

The attack on Pearl happened as the Americans and Japanese were negotiating terms that would supposedly see peace in the Pacific and the attack without a declaration of war or warning was ultimately declared a war crime. The Americans themselves had been preparing for a likely war since the 1920s and Pearl Harbor was designed to remove the American Pacific fleet as a threat so that natural resource-poor Japan could take control of oil, rubber and other resources in British and Dutch colonies. As a result of the aggression shown by the Japanese and to discourage them, the Pacific Fleet was moved from San Diego to Pearl Harbor early in 1941 and the Philippines were sent additional troops and aircraft. Japanese plans were based on the assumption (false, as it turned out) that the US would go to war if Britain's colonies were invaded. However, when the Americans ceased oil exports to Japan in July 1941, they warned the Japanese that they would go to war if the Netherlands Indies were invaded. During 1941, negotiations took place to prevent war, with the Americans wanting a complete Japanese withdrawal from China and the Japanese proposing that they would withdraw from French Indo-China and not attack any British or Dutch possessions if these countries would recommence supplies to Japan. The Japanese war fleet sailed on 26 November and included the following carriers; *Akagi, Kaga, Soryu, Hiryu, Shokaku* and *Zuikaku*. They carried 408 aircraft, with 360 intended for the attack and forty-eight for defence. The pilots were ordered to attack high value targets, mainly the aircraft carriers followed by the battleships and then the cruisers. As well as the surface

Above: Three battleships under attack, from left to right: USS *West Virginia*, severely damaged; USS *Tennessee*, damaged; and USS *Arizona*, sunk.

Upper left: The second wave of Japanese aircraft targeted the aircraft on the ground and many were destroyed. Of the almost 500 aircraft at Pearl Harbor, over two-thirds were either destroyed or badly damaged. These aircraft are at the Ford Island air base.

Bottom left: The remains of a B-17, its tail blown off.

ships, five submarines went with the battle fleet, each carrying a small Type A midget submarine. The five subs had left Kure a day ahead of the main fleet and were within 10 nautical miles of Oahu on 6 December. The submarines were an abject failure though, with one being spotted at 0342 by USS *Condor*. USS *Ward* sank one of the midgets at 0637, making this the first shots fired in the Pacific War by the Americans. One sub fired at USS *St Louis* and USS *Monaghan* but missed and was sunk by the *Monaghan* at 0843. A third midget grounded twice and was captured on 8 December. One of its crew became the first Japanese combatant to become a prisoner of war. The fourth sub was damaged by depth charges before it could fire its torpedoes. In 1999, the last sub was found, in three pieces, but missing its torpedoes. It had radioed to base to confirm firing of its torpedoes at *St Louis* and *Helm*.

The attack was not intended to be a surprise but delays in transcribing coded messages from Japan to its embassy in Washington meant that the declaration was not delivered until after the attack. However, research in the 1990s in Japanese archives show that it was the intention of the Japanese military not to declare war until after the attack.

The first wave of Japanese aircraft, 183 planes, was launched while the carriers were north of Oahu. The American radar detected the incoming bombers but it was assumed they were incoming B-17s that were expected at roughly the same time. By the time the mistake was realised, the Japanese aircraft were already dive-bombing and strafing the base. A second wave hit, with 171 aircraft, and these concentrated on the air bases. Within an hour and a half, the attack was over. 2,008 American sailors were dead and a further 710 wounded. 218 soldiers and army air force crew died too, with 364 wounded. US Marine casualties were 109 killed and sixty-nine wounded. Only sixty-eight civilians died, with thirty-five injured. Five battleships were lost, and another thirteen vessels sunk or severely damaged.

Most casualties took place on the USS *Arizona*. Its forward magazine exploded and she sank with almost all her crew aboard, 1,177 being killed. Of the ships lost and damaged, *Arizona* still remains as a war grave. *Oklahoma* was hit by five torpedoes and capsized, taking 429 crew to their deaths. She was refloated in 1943 and lost when under tow to California in 1947. *West Virginia* was hit by two bombs and seven torpedoes. She was sunk but returned to service in July 1944. *California* was hit by a brace of bombs and torpedoes and also returned to service in 1944. *Nevada* was beached after being hit by six bombs and a torpedo. She was repaired by October 1942. *Tennessee* was repaired and back in service by February 1942, after two bomb hits. *Maryland*, too, was hit by two bombs and reentered service at the same time. *Pennsylvania* was in dry dock and was hit by a solitary bomb and the damage was easily repaired. USS *Utah*, the target ship, capsized and sank after being hit by two torpedoes. Three cruisers, *Helena*, *Raleigh* and *Honolulu*, were damaged, along with the destroyers *Cassin*, *Downes* and *Shaw*. Salvage and repair took many months but six of the eight battleships targeted were returned to service, as did all of the other vessels. Japanese losses were fifty-five aircrew and nine submariners.

Left: Wreckage at Hickam Field, outside the air base's ordnance machine shop.

Below: The burned and twisted wreckage of the USS *Arizona*.

A third Japanese attack was aborted as the ships were at their maximum range and it was unknown where the US carriers were. However, the fact that their carriers were out on exercise certainly saved the Americans from defeat in the Pacific theatre. The loss of HMS *Repulse* and *Prince of Wales* the following week left no major Allied naval units in the Pacific. However, the undisputed truth is that the two elements of the Pacific fleet left untouched by the attack on Pearl Harbor, aircraft carriers and submarines, were exactly the two weapons that won the Pacific war for the Americans. Confidence by the Japanese that the war would be quick meant that they did not attack the infrastructure at Pearl Harbor and this left the dockyard able to repair the damaged ships and to operate fully in support of the Pacific fleet in the coming months and years. The attack was a victory for the Japanese but its very happening caused the Japanese to ultimately lose the war against a determined enemy. The natural resources that Japan so badly needed to wage the war were denied them and by 1945, the amount of imports to Japan to feed their war machine had halved from their 1942 peak.

Right: Three civilians died in this shrapnel-riddled car some 8 miles from Pearl Harbor after a Japanese bomber dropped its load nearby.

Below: President Roosevelt signed the declaration of war against Japan on 8 December 1941, the day after the attack.

Bottom right: The American people woke up that Sunday morning to news of the attack – the first time the USA had been attacked on home soil. San Francisco, 8 December, and newspaper vendors are doing a roaring trade.

Top: The Americans had spotted a midget submarine previous to the aerial attack and had sunk it but the base was still not put on high alert. This view shows the salvage of one of the five two-man submarines after it had been salvaged. *Bottom:* A midget submarine, of the type used at Pearl Harbor, being salvaged in the Solomon Islands.

In November 1941 the British
became aware of the large build-up
of Japanese troops in French Indo-
China, shown on the map above.
The Vichy French were allied to
the Axis powers and had granted
access to the Japanese to the naval
facilities and supplies. The invasion
of Malaya began early in the
morning of 8 December, just before
the attack on Pearl Harbor.

Right: British refugees from
the Malaysian island of Penang
after their arrival at Ipoh on the
peninsula. But their joy may have
been short-lived. Defeat would come
quickly and within two months the
last of the Allied forces had been
evacuated from Malaya.

HMS *Prince of Wales* was launched at Cammell Laird's Birkenhead yard in 1939 and entered service in time for the Atlantic Conference held between Roosevelt and Churchill. With HMS *Revenge*, she was in Malaya as the Japanese invaded and was lost on 10 December 1941 when attacked by Japanese aircraft.

Left: She is shown here with HMS *Revenge* while trying to evade the bombs dropped by the Japanese. 327 died as she sank.

Top right: Soldiers of the 2nd Argyll & Sutherland Highlanders in Malaya. The men fought fiercely to slow down the Japanese advance southwards through Malaya to Singapore.

Middle right: Australian soldiers drafted to Singapore. They couldn't stem the tide of the Japanese invasion forces and by mid-February 1942 Singapore had fallen.

Bottom right: Engineers are placing explosives to mine a bridge at Kuala Lumpur, the capital of Malaya, or as the country is now known, Malaysia.

By 7 December 1941, Tobruk was finally relieved by the 8th Army, consisting of British, Indian, New Zealand and South African troops, and by 24 December British forces had captured Benghazi. *Above:* British infantry moving up through the barbed wire at Tobruk. *Below:* The tangled wreckage of a German lorry in the Western Desert.

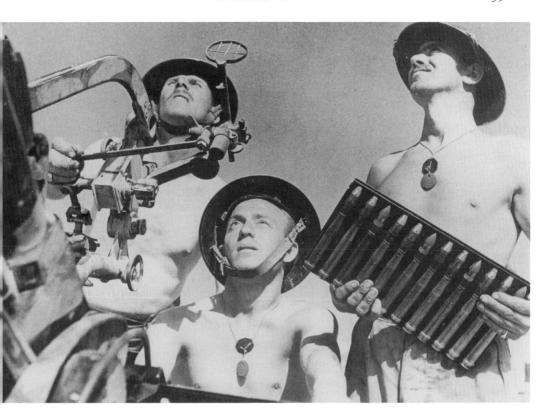

Top: Gunners manning a captured Italian Breda 20-mm anti-aircraft gun. *Bottom:* One of the impregnable British bunkers at Tobruk.

Pilots of No. 257, the famous Hurricane squadron adopted by Burma. In 1940 the squadron had taken part in the Battle of Britain as part of No. 11 Group based at RAF Northolt, and in 1941 it began sweeps into northern France. In the lower image, Squadron Leader Stanford Tuck is shown in the cockpit of one of the Hurricanes with the Burmese flag painted on its side.